If you want to create a
to start by creating a
book is about.

Giovanna D'Alessio provides a step by step process for understanding yourself and becoming the master of your destiny rather than the victim of your fears.

Richard Barrett, Author, The New Leadership Paradigm

In these turbulent times, the ability of people to self-actualize and self-empower is the way to create the shift in the collective consciousness required for evolving as humans beings. *Personal Mastery: The Path to Transformative Leadership* provides a process for liberating ourselves from the fears and the unconscious programming of our childhood so we can step into our highest potential as leaders."

Marcia Reynolds, PsyD, author of "Wander Woman - How High-Achieving Women Find Contentment and Direction"

Giovanna D'Alessio is an innovator in the field of executive coaching. She has a gift for bringing out the best in her work with CEOs and other senior leaders of the global companies who engage her services. Now, in this book, she shares this gift with you. Highly recommended!

Michael J. Gelb, author, How to Think Like Leonardo da Vinci.

PERSONAL MASTERY

The Path to Transformative Leadership

Giovanna D'Alessio

Published in 2014

First printing: 2014

ISBN n. 978-88-909576-1-1

Publishing company:
Asterys s.r.l.
Via di Villa Zingone, 36
Rome, Italy 00151

www.asterys.com

To my soul mate and business partner Pier Paolo,
who inspires me and teaches me
to stay in a path of consciousness.

Summary

Foreword

By Sir John Whitmore[1]

I recently met and had good conversation with Giovanna in South Africa. We found much to agree about and I am happy to write this Foreword for her book. She very well addresses many matters in our daily lives that our schools do not cover, most people do not think about, or realize that they can influence and improve. Giovanna raises deep and important issues in ways that are very clear and understandable for ordinary people to improve the qualities of their inner lives.
Human beings tend to become 'programmed' by their parents, friends, schools, and community and social behaviors and beliefs. They just believe that that is how life is, and that it will probably be so

---

[1] Sir John Whitmore is pre-eminent authority in coaching and organizational change and works with multinational companies to develop a managerial coaching culture and leadership programs through the company which he is President: Performance Consultants International. Former professional driver, he has left the world of motorsport to apply its expertise to the world of business. He has written five books on leadership, coaching and sports, of which *Coaching* is the most famous, with half a million copies sold in 17 languages.

forever. They are not taught that individuals, society and humanity are evolving. Of course the psycho-social evolution is relatively slow but individuals can develop themselves personally and quite quickly. Sadly this is seldom taught to or understood by, most of us.
Giovanna's book deals with this issue very well and very accessibly and I would advise many people to read it – twice would be a good idea! Although at this time humanity is facing several crises, economic, environmental, food, transport and greedy materialism, this is also an opportunity for change. This is helped today by the fact that many old beliefs are failing and are wrong. We need to rethink about our wants and needs, and what brings us and others joy.
To successfully enjoy a new life we need to unlearn old or false beliefs in order to create the space for new ideas and ways of thinking and living. Giovanna's book will help people well to join new and often exciting lifestyles and journeys. She addresses this in three parts, 'Getting ready for the Journey', 'Knowing yourself' and 'Personal Transformation'.

Read on and have a great journey for the rest of your life!

Introduction

"... I am what I am, I cannot change." I have heard this phrase many times, especially from people who have had a great influence on me and played a role in my development. I have always refused to accept such a limiting belief. Yet I realize that the resistance to change in every human being, including myself, is so strong that often we are likely to remain in a cocoon of choices that are unexciting but risk-free, at least at first sight.

●●●

"What we call our destiny is in reality our character, and the character can change."
Anaïs Nin.

●●●

What happens when we take this direction, and choose to remain in a "safety zone", is that life seems to put in front of us situations and relationships whose twisted or unwanted mechanism repeats itself continuously – situation after situation, relationship after relationship. Did you ever think about the fact that the men (or women) we are drawn to and with whom we have relations are always incredibly similar, and the complications

and motivations behind the split up are so predictable? And yet we fall for it time and time again?
Or has it ever happened that you had wanted to change jobs or company to escape a situation that was unhealthy for you (for example, a destructive relationship with your boss) and then find yourself in a new workplace facing similar problems? It feels like being in the movie Nirvana by Gabriele Salvatores, in which, because of a computer virus, the protagonist of a computer game, Solo (played by Italian actor Diego Abatantuono) becomes conscious that he exists. Solo realizes he is trapped in the repetition of his pseudo-life because he always relives the same scene. To end this endless sequence, Solo asks his creator (the programmer of the game) to eliminate him.
What happens to us, in real life, is quite similar to what happens to Solo, and in most cases we are not aware of this infernal closed-loop system, until something happens - an event, a feeling, a sudden realization - that makes us take a quantum leap in our awareness.
But unlike Solo, who sees no option but his own elimination if he is to end the spiraling of his virtual existence, the human being is able to evolve and make personal transformations that allow him to break the pattern and create the life and the circumstances he wants.
In the first thirty five years of my life, even though I felt annoyed by the fatalistic line "But I am what I am …" (or even worse "What can you do? You are who you are...", which boxed me into the category of those who cannot change, and are destined to immobility), I cannot say that I actively explored the domain of transformation and personal evolution. My family has always been outspokenly agnostic and nothing that had a spiritual flavor was

contemplated. Wikipedia defines agnosticism - from the Greek a-gnothein aka "not knowing" - as "a conceptual position in which one suspends the judgment with respect to a problem because he has not - or he cannot have – enough knowledge". But when I reflect on that meaning, I realize that there wasn't any suspended judgment, but criticism and sarcasm toward any spiritual matters. We were open to consider only what could be proven scientifically.

I would never have faced a personal transformation journey like the one I subsequently accomplished (and that I continue every day) if the various branches of science had not made key strides in recent decades, and if there hadn't been the convergence and cross-pollination of different disciplines - from neuroscience to quantum mechanics, from emotional intelligence to transpersonal psychology, from biology to cardiology - that I've studied to expand my awareness. Finally, after years of limiting certainties, I started to know I didn't know.

So the skeptic in me began to consider other visions of reality without immediately discarding them as "New Age stuff ". Perhaps what science is discovering today is throwing a bridge between the scientific and the spiritual world.

What is happening is that, in many ways, scientific discoveries in various fields seem to want to give us a new vision on how man and the world in which he lives work. Quantum mechanics, for example, in its scientific experiments shows that we have much more influence on our lives that we have been used to thinking, particularly in the Western world. The switch from "But I am who I am..." to "I'm the one deciding who I want to be..." is not that crazy, after all. Neuroscience begins to explore the "not-local" connection between human beings - as it happens, for example, in the phenomenon of distance connection - and to provide us with some explanation.

Epigenetics is opening our eyes to the possibility that the expression of the genetic inheritance of man can be the product of the interaction with the environment and that the changes made by it can be passed on to future generations.

The book you are about to read is intended as a journey through the possibility of what these new findings may offer us human beings if we are able to understand their meaning, and also as a journey of self-discovery, of the immeasurable potential we possess, in order to gain a complete personal mastery and to fully express our leadership. The term leadership in this book has the meaning of personal excellence, an authentic expression of the inner life of the person. It is therefore applicable to managers of small and large companies and also to all those who want to manage themselves and the people around them better, even if only their own families.

Albert Einstein famously said: "We cannot solve problems with the same level of consciousness with which we created them." I imagine that humanity advances in an upward spiral. The development of the human being is an emergent process in which new paradigms and behavioral systems of a higher order override old paradigms and behavioral systems of lower orders. Clearly we have a powerful and dynamic mind that can recalibrate in response to new conditions and also reorganize itself in a new way.

Clare W. Graves, a famous American professor of psychology - whose theories on the cyclical evolution of the human existence have inspired the Spiral Dynamics model - states that "... As man solves existential problems on one level, new

systems in the brain may be activated and, when activated, they will change his perception, in order to show him new problems of life."
So, to evolve along the spiral and solve problems that we created with a lower level of awareness, we need to expand awareness itself. This is one of the purposes of this book: to provide you with some ideas to help you change your perception and look at yourself from a new level of consciousness.

In my work as an executive coach and facilitator of transformation,
I support leaders of large organizations and help them to become aware of what causes their unintended results, to analyze their paradigms and mindsets; I challenge them to give their mindsets and paradigms away to see the situation that they want to change with entirely new eyes. Often the change is about the entire culture of the organization.
Concepts such as those explained in the book, and also some exercises, are the ingredients of many transformational interventions that I deliver with other coaches and facilitators in organizations or groups. Through the written words, I hope to evoke the energy that is palpable in each workshop and that guides participants toward a deep shift in their awareness. Some of the comments we most frequently receive are on these lines:

> *"It was really exciting and enjoyable to start this path together with Giovanna and Pier Paolo. I could immediately touch with hand and with satisfaction important positive transformations on how I live my personal and working life. It is an experience that I would really recommend*

to anyone who wishes to live his life authentically!" Massimo – Entrepreneur

"A wonderful experience of emotions and relationships. You get out of those three days, and things will seem completely different and... there is no going back!" Simona - Head of HR

"A place where there is love, where no one judges, where everybody helps you, where you can express your emotions openly, where every minute is a moment of life, where you dialogue with people who are searching for their transformation. Here's what the workshop was for me. It allowed me to start a powerful process of transformation that will never end." Jose - Consultant

I wanted this book to integrate the knowledge of the possibilities that new scientific discoveries can open to the human being, the timeless teachings of the Eastern philosophies, and the experience of years of work on personal and organizational transformations to give you food for thought, challenge your vision of yourself and the world, and provide you with tools and exercises to transform your way of being and become the master of your life.

HOW TO USE THIS BOOK

In any real evolutionary path, learning does not emerge from the cognitive understanding of concepts and theories, but from practical experimentation and a deep and genuine inner quest. I suggest reflections, exercises, paths of investigation for each topic. If you want to browse through the pages of the book, skip the discussion points and then close it again and say "I am who I am," if you're not open or ready to see yourself and your life in a different way, I suggest not to invest time and money. The book does not have magical powers but, like anything in life, you will derive from it what you are willing to invest.

If instead you want to undertake a path of true discovery of yourself, if you are ready to invest time and energy in it, if you're willing to question your assumptions, then perhaps this is the right time to read this book. Throughout the journey it will be very helpful to arm yourself with a notebook to use for the exercises and to write down your thoughts.

One suggestion for dealing more effectively with this journey is to share it with someone as interested in personal transformation as you are. You can do the exercises as a couple, supporting each other and making yourselves mutually responsible for the commitments that you make (like when you go to the gym with a friend... there is mutual encouragement).

You can also consider the idea of creating a study group, involve two or more people working together, sharing and discussing the various points of view that each participant brings to the group. I assure you that the group multiplies the possibilities of learning and it becomes a very deep growth experience.

One last tip. I will explain the easiest way I can some theories and the results of scientific experiments. I do not have a degree in physics or biology or neurology, but I have explored these issues with passion and interest. For me the important thing is to present information that may be of support to a journey of transformation.

And this program works whether you understand the underlying scientific laws or not. If science is not your forte, do not worry (Richard Feynman, Nobel Prize winner for the development of quantum electrodynamics, said: "I think I can say with confidence that no one understands quantum mechanics"). It is not necessary to completely understand all the theory before starting your journey. Follow the reflections and exercises as your heart and head suggest.

One last note. My intention is to address both universes, male and female. In the text, I will use sometimes the feminine third person and sometimes the masculine to avoid having to use the double form (him/her, his/her, etc..). I look for your comments and your thoughts on www.giovannadalessio.com.

Part I: Getting Ready For the Journey

1.Open Mind

•••
The real voyage of discovery consists not in seeking new landscapes but in having new eyes.
Marcel Proust
•••

Entirely new concepts for you, such as those you might find in this book, could put a strain on the deeply held paradigms and prejudices that form the basis of your world view. The paradigms are mostly unconscious and characterize our modus operandi.
Whenever we come across something new, by definition this is something that represents for us a discontinuity with the past. It does not resemble anything that we already know. This discontinuity may surprise and thrill us and or it can disorient and frighten us.
If the second effect is the one that prevails, then we will use our paradigms to deny and criticize this new information just because it does not fit with

what we take for granted. In order to have new learning it is important to be open to consider new points of view, to question what for us has been the undeniable reality so far (we will see in subsequent chapters that what we mean by "reality" is just an illusion). We must therefore approach the new with an open mind.

●●●

Your paradigm is so intrinsic to your mental processes that you are hardly aware of their existence. Until you try to communicate with someone who has a different paradigm.
Donella Meadow

●●●

The first basic step in our journey is to train ourselves to recognize what are our paradigms and to maintain an open mind to the possibilities of bringing awareness to a higher level. A paradigm is a mental model that allows those who adopt it to interpret and use new information. It is the general point of view from which we observe the world. It shapes what we observe, how we perceive things, which problems we decide to tackle and how we deal with them. And it does so in an almost totally unconscious and unchallenging way. Paradigms are a way to filter and give meaning to all information that bombards us daily[2] .

A classic example of change of paradigm is offered to us by Copernicus. When the vision of Copernicus - the sun at the center of the universe – was finally accepted, it fully overturned astronomy as it was conceived, that is, the prevailing paradigm at the time. The geocentric system collapsed under the weight of the information that the old paradigm could not explain, and a whole series of problems

---

2 John Darwin, Phil Johnson, John McAuley, *Developing Strategies for Change*, Prentice Hall/Financial Times, 2002.

and ideas, which until then had been considered important, lost meaning.

The new heliocentric thinking made mankind jump to that higher level of consciousness that Einstein mentions in his famous quote. The heliocentric view is therefore a new paradigm that undermines the previous and commonly accepted one. In the case of the heliocentric theory, Copernicus' assertions not only challenged the concept of astronomy of the time, but their anthropological and sociological effects contrasted the whole philosophical and religious systems (think of what it meant then to find that the earth is not the center of the universe and the celestial and terrestrial phenomena are subject to the same mathematical and physical laws).

But in addition to scientific paradigms, which when they challenge or replace earlier ones can cause an explosive change in the global perspective of humanity, there are also the paradigms that govern our personal lives (individual paradigms) and the life of our community or culture (group paradigms). We adopt paradigms in various areas of our human activities and make assumptions regarding expectations with respect to what could happen.

A very famous example concerns a man who in the forties showed up at the lab of a well-known company in the field of photography to illustrate a new photographic process. He showed the manager a red box with a steel plate, a charging device, a light bulb and a container of black powder. No camera, no film, no darkroom. The printed photograph was weak but readable. The managers who expected to see the classic materials and tools of photography, didn't understand the value and missed the opportunity to embrace the new process of electrostatic

photography (or EP), which proved to be a multi-billion dollar industry: copiers.
When the information we receive (the man with his red box) falls outside of our paradigm ("to take a photograph you need a camera, film and a darkroom") we are hardly able to see, let alone accept, the information. This is what is called the "paradigm effect". And when the paradigm effect is strong enough to keep us from seeing what is before our eyes, we say we suffer from "paradigm paralysis".
This kind of paralysis is common in communities or companies that have been around for many years, and which over time have developed ways of working and interacting with one another that have grown into a "culture", or group paradigm. Have you ever tried to propose a new idea when you are a new employee in a well-established organization only to have it criticized or rejected because: "We have our own way of doing things here"? Such a response sounds terribly like "This is who I am".
When a paradigm or mindset has worked in the past, it becomes indisputable, even if external (or internal) conditions have completely changed.

THE PARADIGM OF THE PUNISHED MONKEY

How a group mindset comes into being is beautifully illustrated by an experiment conducted several years ago in the United States by a group of scientists who studied the behavior of a group of monkeys.
Five monkeys were kept in a cage. At the center of the cage was placed a ladder and on top of the ladder a bunch of bananas. When the monkeys saw the bananas they tried to climb the ladder.
At this point, the scientists inserted a mechanism causing any monkey who climbed the ladder to

generate a shower of cold water on the rest of the monkeys. After a few cold showers the monkeys understood the link between climbing the ladder and cold water.

From that moment every time one of them tried to approach the stairs, she would be attacked and beaten by the others. After several attempts, the monkeys gave up trying to climb, despite the temptation of bananas.

At this stage scientists introduced two variations in the experiment. The cold water punishment was eliminated and one of the monkeys was replaced with a newcomer who hadn't taken part in the earlier phase of the experiment. Seeing the bananas, the new monkey approached the ladder to climb it and take them. The four monkeys who had experienced the icy water immediately beat the new monkey, who could not figure out why she was being beaten. After a few attempts the newcomer began to adapt and gave up the bananas.

The scientists then introduced a second new monkey to replace another of the original group. This new monkey tried to climb the ladder and take the bananas. At that point, guess what happened? That's right, the monkey was severely beaten not only by the three who had been inflicted with the cold water shower the first few times, but also by the one who had not lived through that experience and therefore had no idea why she was beating her.

The experiment went on until all the monkeys were replaced and all were beaten in every attempt to approach the ladder. In the end what remained was a group of five monkeys who had never suffered the punishment of the cold water but who avoided climbing the ladder to take the bananas and beat any monkey who dared to do so.

This experiment provides tragic food for thought about how the corporate or community culture gets shaped and how “the way things are done” becomes established. Unwritten rules are respected and new ideas are rejected without a reason, but only because “things have always been done this way.”
From collective paradigms let’s move on to individual ones. Our life is practically governed by our paradigms. Maybe these are concepts we were taught or beliefs we have developed.
Certainly they help us to maintain consistency in our values and our behavior. And often they are useful. If we were to take into consideration all the possibilities available to us each time we decided whether to take a coffee at breakfast, it would not be very functional.
But if we are not aware of the paradigms that guide our lives and we are not able to suspend them to take different paradigms into account, our growth as human beings will be extremely limited. Each change can become intolerable and an event to be avoided at all costs.
But if the paradigms are mostly unconscious, how do we become aware of them?
We must begin to develop the ability to observe ourselves with a certain detachment, as if we looked at someone else, and ask questions that might reveal some traces of our paradigms.
I'll give you some examples of the paradigms that have long guided my life. "Homeopathic medicine does not work. Instead you take a tablet and the pain goes away." (I have never studied this discipline in depth; I have not seen surveys or research, so ... where does this belief come from?).
"Man is alone in this world, and death is nothing more than the end, there is nothing left but dust and bits of bone." (Until a few years ago I had never

considered - or tried to understand - what religions and philosophies have to say about afterlife or reincarnation. Can it be that I always heard this sentence in my family?).
"Women find affirmation only through work and financial independence." (How can I be so sure? What impact has this paradigm had in my life? Is this the reason why I've been successful in my job but I don't have children?). "I need to have everything under control to make sure things are done well." (But who said that? What a pain it has been and sometimes still is - even when we are aware of paradigms, they can be so deeply rooted that it is not easy to get rid of them – to keep everything under control! Could I let myself go a little bit more and see if the catastrophe that I expect really happens?).
These are just a few examples from different areas of my life. But now it's up to you.

Reflection: What are your paradigms?
It is easier to detect a paradigm when we are in contact with someone who has a different one. It is then that we tend to defend our paradigm, because if it is challenged we feel thrown off balance. That moment - the confrontation with a different paradigm - is a good opportunity to recognize our own.
Think, therefore, about various important issues in your life and about the times in which you discussed those issues, perhaps with a loved one.
A belief you held blindly without necessarily having a "scientific" basis for doing so. Ask yourself, "What is the paradigm that underlies this fundamental belief?".
For each area of your life, find the paradigm that colors and influences your attitude.

Life themes	**Paradigms**
Family	
Children's education	
Death	
Success	
Making money	
Health	
Ethics	
Good manners	
Friendship	
Showing emotions at work	
What matters in life	

Read what you wrote again. Did you find anything interesting? Perhaps there is a paradigm that has

had (and maybe still has) a particular role in how you have looked at your life and your world and has influenced your choices?
We reflect on our paradigms not necessarily to deny them or to throw them away, but to recognize and acknowledge the role they have had in the choices we have made. The paradigms will come back into play in a few chapters.

THE BEGINNER'S MIND

The ideas of Copernicus, whose heliocentric theory we mentioned before, were certainly not welcomed with an open mind by everyone, so much so that his work (De Revolutionibus Orbium Coelestium), written in 1514, was printed only in the month of his death almost thirty years later, in 1543.

●●●

"In the beginner's mind there are many possibilities, but in the expert's there are few."
Shunryu Suzuki

●●●

Thomas Samuel Kuhn, an American philosopher (1922-1996), writing about individuals who make discoveries that generate a new paradigm, said that they are:

> *almost always [...] or very young or very new in the field of which they are to change the paradigm [...] These are men [and women] who, being little affected and faithful to the traditional rules, are more likely to succeed to see that those rules no longer define a sustainable system and to conceive another set of rules that can replace them.*

In the world of advertising, for example, when the creative team gets "stuck" and fails to generate good, intriguing and memorable ideas to advertise a product, it is often because they have long known about both the product and the client company and have developed some paradigms around the way they work, what pleases the customer, and so on. Until a new creative team is called in, with a “fresh mind”, whose members don’t know the product and therefore don’t have preconceptions or prejudices, it is hard to keep generating creative ideas. We can say that scientists such as Copernicus or the creative teams we just mentioned - or ourselves when we have good ideas – look at the issue they face with a "beginner's mind" as suggested by the Zen Master Shunryu Suzuki.
Having a "beginner's mind" means possessing a mind free of preconceptions and expectations, judgments and prejudices. It means being awake, exploring and observing things as they are. And this state of mind is a pre-condition for learning.

There is a famous Zen story that illustrates the beginner’s mind.

> *A university professor went to visit a famous Zen master. While the master quietly served tea, the professor talked about Zen. The master poured the visitor's cup to the brim, and then kept pouring. The professor watched the overflowing cup until he could no longer restrain himself. "It's overfull! No more will go in!" the professor blurted. "You are like this cup," the master replied, "How can I show you Zen unless you first empty your cup?"*

Emptying our mind of all preconceptions, ideas, techniques and methods that prevent us from learning something new seems an easy task, but in practice it is very difficult. And we must not only make sure that our cup is empty, but that it is also clean, so that we don't find some "taste" of the old substances it has held.
Another important element is to get rid of the "seen it, done it" attitude. It may be true that you have done or seen something like this before, but maybe your past learning is not necessarily complete. I have experienced firsthand how this attitude may limit learning. I started to deliver in-class training at the age of twenty-two, when the director of the school of communication I attended sent me to speak to a group of marketing executives at the Italian Institute for Foreign Trade. During the fifteen years since then, though it hasn't been my main activity, I have delivered training in various institutes, companies and organizations. When I left the corporate world to devote myself to coaching and facilitation, I deepened my studies on adult learning and change. I then developed some experience in classroom training, teaching techniques, and learning theories.
The first time I witnessed a transformational workshop as a student, I immediately adopted the "seen it, done it" attitude and spent the first day and a half criticizing the trainers and the methodology without learning anything (which of course confirmed my belief that I had seen and done this before and that there was nothing to learn). At the end of the second day something happened that suddenly reversed this attitude: I had a couple of insights, deep realizations about myself and about my behavior that allowed me to make a leap forward in my self-awareness.

I was on a path toward learning to deliver that kind of workshop and provoke the same profound transformation in the awareness of the participants. That workshop was only the first step: I had to experience the workshop before I could learn to deliver it. In the sixty days of training, my eleven colleagues and I practiced the delivery of each workshop module several times, playing the part either of the facilitator or of the participant. That meant that each of us attended the modules at least a dozen times. Having learned the lesson of "beginner's mind", however, I attended each session as if it were my first. And I had an interesting surprise: every single time, I witnessed the emergence of new insights and learning.

I invite you to try doing a simple exercise in observation. Choose a time when you can have a long conversation with someone, perhaps a person you know and who wants to tell you about a new theory or a new infallible diet. Or with a co-worker of yours who comes to tell you about an idea to change some business processes.

Observe yourself while you listen and notice every time you:

- judge what he says
- ignore the reasons or explanations he gives in support of the idea or theory
- make assumptions about what he means without wanting to get a better understanding
- think "yeah, that's happened to me, I know what that's like"
- have thoughts like, "I already know this won't work", "it would be nice but there's no budget", "I did something similar last month/ last year" and so on
- answer with something like "yes, it's like the Zone Diet" (or the dissociated diet, or the project we designed a decade ago; in short try

to bring the idea or project back to something you know and are familiar with)
- think you have a better, more efficient, cheaper idea

Whenever you notice any of these internal processes, make a gesture you've decided beforehand (for example move a hand). I do not suggest you do this so as to look like a fool, but simply to have a visible amplifier to show you how many times during a conversation your "expert" mind hinders the possibility of considering a new thing.
Once you get used to noticing these interferences you can make the decision to eliminate them. You just need to notice them coming, acknowledge them, and imagine temporarily putting them on a hanger or in a drawer.

TOWARD A NEW PARADIGM OF THE HUMAN NATURE

The paradigms that in the last four hundred years have underlined scientific thought and research, and which have influenced – and continue to influence - the vision of what is possible and what is not, are the materialistic and mechanistic models of reality.
In these models, the universe is like a machine composed of solid material elements, and reality is what is measurable, what we can perceive with our five senses. This machine must be seen and studied with objective and emotionless methods.
According to this Newtonian view, the universe is mechanical and predictable. Perhaps it was once created by some form of intelligence but now, once set in motion, is regulated by specific laws which,

given a series of initial conditions, predetermine the outcome of any event.
The human being is then divided into body (a mechanism) and mind (a mere epiphenomenon, that is, a "side effect" to which science has devoted little or no attention). Emotions, intuition and imagination are not valued, while cognitive and rational processes are glorified.
Where does life lead us, according to this vision? The human being wanders aimlessly in a constant struggle for survival, in a world where nature is subjugated to man and everything is determined and predictable, and consequently there is no freedom of choice.
This paradigm is demeaning and degrading. It leads to a sense of helplessness and encourages an attitude of irresponsibility. If everything is determined and my choices have no impact on the world, then I just have to take advantage as far as I can of this life, and who cares if I'm robbing natural resources, or abusing my neighbor... after all everything is inevitable. In this paradigm it is consistent to say "...That's just how I am, I cannot change ". Man also is a machine, and it has to be accepted that he doesn't take responsibility for his behaviors and their consequences. The Newtonian view is the cause of so much suffering, conflict, poverty, injustice. In this paradigm, consciousness and soul have no place. These elements have been delegated to religion. Because they cannot be codified and are less important, they have no place in the old scientific view. And certain other phenomena cannot be explained either, even though they have been talked about for a long time, such as out of body or near-death experiences, the phenomena of mental healing, or heart transplant recipients acquiring the tastes and preferences of

the donor, an observation made by doctors in many cases.

Millions of people in the world (particularly the West, since the Eastern world is driven by other paradigms) look with hope to the discoveries of scientific disciplines, such as quantum mechanics, neuroscience, biology, psychology. These disciplines seem now to be converging toward a non-dualistic vision of the world, in which the material is not divided from the mind, where "internal" and "external" reality are not separated from each other, where everything is interconnected, where man exercises his free will, and where the human being lives to accomplish a purpose.

I do not know if it is people, under certain conditions of hardship, who influence scientific disciplines, forcing them to focus on certain areas in order to discover new theories. Or if the progress of science inevitably leads to the subordination of old theories with new. The fact is that I feel we stand on the edge of a new paradigm, one that can provide the human individual with a greater power of choice and a broader sense of life's meaning.

It is not even a new paradigm. From the Hindu tradition to Buddhism to the Kabbalah, from the beliefs of the indigenous people of Latin America to those of the American Indians, the majority of ancient religious and philosophical traditions have a common denominator, that is, a unitary concept of the human being (body, mind, soul) in a relationship of oneness with the universe. It seems that humanity is simply returning home, after gaining knowledge of the matter, and drawing closer to the point of integrating the parts that must coexist for a life to have meaning.

The important thing is to have an open mind, to analyze reality with both mind and heart, and always ask ourselves questions that can pave the way for an expansion of our awareness.

THE DISRUPTION OF THE CERTAINTY OF CLASSICAL PHYSICS

At the end of the nineteenth century, classical physics seemed to approach the condition of a perfect theory, but the models that until then had served to explain the behavior of things in the material world have proven ineffective in tiny and huge dimensions, and in high speed interactions.

●●●
"If quantum mechanics hasn't profoundly shocked you, you haven't understood it yet."
Niels Bohr
●●●

Quantum mechanics (or quantum theory) is that part of physics that has to do with matter and energy on a very small scale. I mean, the size of atoms and subatomic particles or waves. The term was coined by Max Born in 1924 (the word quantum derives from Latin and means "unit of quantity").

Although at first ignored and opposed by classical physicists (even Einstein invested a lot of his time trying to disprove quantum theory), the subsequent acceptance of this branch of physics was possible thanks to its accurate prediction of the physical behavior of systems, including those to which Newtonian mechanics couldn't be applied.

There are some basic ideas in quantum mechanics that we will explore here for the philosophical consequences that arise regarding the way human beings see themselves in the world and the possibilities that can open up for humanity:

1. Neither vacuums nor solid matter exist, there is only energy.

2. The observer affects the nature of what is observed.
3. Particles that enter into relationship remain connected even after being separated.

At first glance it may seem like a far-fetched theory, but in reality it gives us an idea of the possible nature of the universe and tells us that it is completely different from the world that we have before our eyes. As Niels Bohr, one of the fathers of quantum mechanics, observed: "If quantum mechanics hasn't profoundly shocked you, you haven't understood it yet."
Let's then explore what new points of view it offers us.

1. Vacuum does not exist, there is only energy
Quantum mechanics has shown that vacuum does not exist. According to the Uncertainty Principle developed by Heisenberg in 1926, in fact, it is impossible to know in the same moment, and with the maximum precision, both position and speed of an electron. This implies that no particle ever completely stops but it is in a continuous movement due to an energy field that interacts constantly with all the subatomic matter. In the vicinity of the absolute zero then the space is not empty, but is filled with electromagnetic fluctuations, which means that the basic structure of the universe is a sea of energy.
If this understanding of the zero-point field was included in our conception of the fundamental nature of matter, the essence and the unifying element of our universe would, then, be a sea of energy. Everything would be connected with everything else as an invisible network and we humans would relate with everyone else, and with the world.

The experiments around the zero-point field suggest that there could be a "life force" that flows through the universe and this would represent a scientific explanation of philosophical and metaphysical concepts such as Jung's collective unconscious, the "qi" of the Chinese or, in religious terms, the spirit.

2. The observer affects the nature of what is observed

The duality between particles and waves is one of the main findings of quantum mechanics. Through numerous experiments from the end of the nineteenth century, it was shown, first with light and later with electrons, that they will act as particles one moment, in another as waves, according to how they are being observed. One of the most interesting experiments in this area is the one conducted by the American physicist and Nobel Prize winner Richard Feynman in 1962 (see box below).

At the time of the first experiments, the physicists were literally shocked by what they were discovering and were unable to explain it.

PARTICLE OR WAVE?
THE DOUBLE-SLIT EXPERIMENT

In Feynman's 1962 experiment, electrons (negatively charged particles outside the nucleus of the atom) were "fired" against a wall where the impact of such particles could be recorded. In front of the wall was placed a plate with two slits through which the electrons were fired. Instead of seeing, on the back wall, a series of points corresponding with the slits through which particles had passed (as you might intuitively expect), the arrival points of the electrons were distributed in a pattern of interference, characteristic of waves (as shown in Figure 1.1). In other words, although assumed to be individual particles, electrons reached the target as if they were waves. As soon as a device was introduced that was able to read which slit an electron was passing through, the electrons abandoned the wave behavior and manifested solely as particles (Figure 1.2).

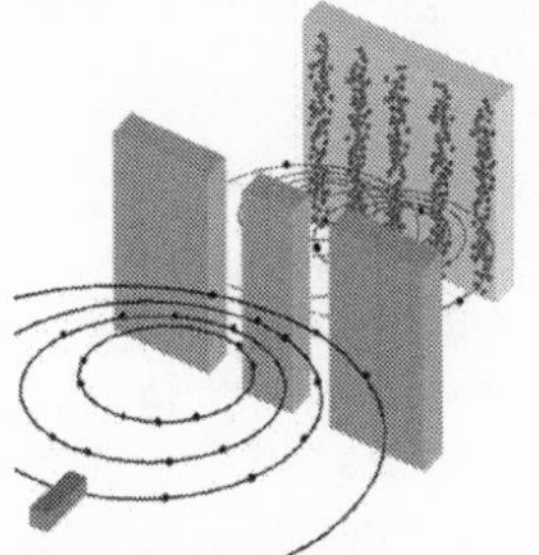

***Figure 1.1:** Wave Interference Pattern*

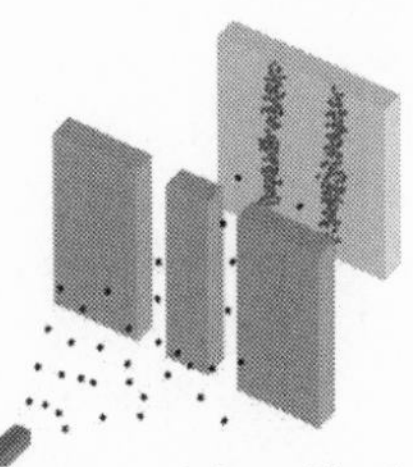

***Figure 1.2:** Electrons fired through two slits with a system to detect through which slit they passed.*

In summary: when individual electrons were detected they behaved as particles - moving in one slit and distributing on the wall in correspondence of the slit where they have gone through - and when they were not detected they behave like waves, passing through both the slits and then interfering with themselves.

Ultimately, then, before being observed the electron exists as a probability, capable of behaving as a particle and at the same time as a wave, and then, in being observed, "collapses" into only one of these. In other words, therefore, the act of observation attributes to the electron a single characteristic from among those to which it has potential access.

Max Born offered a reading of this phenomenon, according to which the wave associated with a particle is a wave of "probability", in the sense that it "prescribes" the possible futures for that particle. The state of a particle is given by the superposition of all its possible futures, each one "weighted" according to its probability. When we insert a meter or an "observer", then the electron "decides" to act in one way or another and between the various probabilities only one is manifested.
Niels Bohr, who worked around 1927 in Copenhagen, presented what was then called the Copenhagen Interpretation of quantum theory, namely that the electron is whichever the observer decides to measure, either wave or particle. When the observer looks for a particle, a particle is revealed. When instead the observer looks for a wave, a wave is revealed.
In other words, what the observer decides to measure affects the behavior of the electron, which exists in potential both as a wave and as a particle until the observation makes it "collapse" (i.e. manifests in one form or another), forcing it to choose only one path.
Bohr extended the reasoning and stated that nature loves to keep all options open, and therefore to follow every possible path. Only when observed is it forced to choose one path, to take a single road.
What then is the "reality" of the world in quantum physics? At first glance it may seem that it is just a series of arbitrary moments in a universe in which crazy electrons live in a state of probability until they choose to collapse, and make something happen. The sequence of those "somethings" is the reality we perceive.
But what causes the collapse of an electron? Is anything capable of prompting such a collapse by

performing an act of observation, or is it only the human mind that can cause this phenomenon?

3. Particles that come into contact remain connected after separation

In 1982, Alain Aspect, a French physicist, conducted an experiment which showed that particles are closely related at a level beyond time and space and thus escape the known laws of physics. He also demonstrated that objects influence each other remotely. In this experiment two photons, A and B, generated by the decay of an atom of calcium, travel in two different directions. When, subsequently, particle A deviates from its path, particle B, now at a distance, deflects in the same way.

Aspect's study demonstrates that particles are connected in ways that we do not understand. Every particle "knows" what the other particles, with which it has previously interacted, are doing.

In 1994, a researcher at the University of Mexico, Jacobo Grinberg-Zylberbaum, wanted to verify if this capacity was also extended to humans. Grinberg-Zylberbaum spent three years experimenting with the ability of the brain to maintain a remote connection. In his experiments, he selected two students and made them focus on each other for some time. Then he took student A into a dark room, which was electromagnetically screened to prevent disturbances or cheating, and connected him to an electroencephalograph (EEG) which recorded brain activity and to other machinery.

He took student B to a dark, screened room in another part of the University and connected him also to various machines including the electroencephalograph. The experiment involved administering very strong stimuli to student A, such as an intense beam of light or a very loud noise. The brain of student A responded to these stimuli and the EEG recorded peaks of activity. Meanwhile, student B was sitting quietly in his room, not receiving any stimulus. According to his EEG, however, though he was unconscious of it, his brain was undergoing changes similar to those of student A. When the two EEG readings were synchronized in time and compared, there was a direct correlation between the stimulus inflicted on student A's brain and the unconscious response of Student B. The two brains were in some sort of connection although neither of them was aware of what was happening to the other.

An experiment conducted more recently by Cleve Backster on behalf of the U.S. military forces is even more intriguing. White blood cells from different donors were collected and placed in containers where changes to them could be measured. Each donor was then escorted to a different room to watch videos, which had the aim of stimulating emotional reactions. The containers with the leukocytes were placed in different rooms, separate from each other and from their donors. From monitoring the donors and the relative containers of leukocytes, research highlighted that as soon as the donor manifested changes in his emotional state, as detected by the electrical measurements, the leukocytes reacted in the same way and at the same moment, without any time lag. Surprised by these results, the researcher varied the experiment by placing donor leukocytes at a much greater distance, up to 80 km apart, and the results were the same: changes of emotional intensity in the donor were equivalent to changes in the leukocytes, without any time delay.

Can our cells communicate through a form of energy that is not subject to time and distance?

Could this non-local energy be the "zero-point field" or something like it? Is there a different dimension beyond the five senses? What kind of new light is shed on human abilities and on phenomena such as intuition or premonition by this possibility of our being connected in a non-local way?

THE CREATIVE POTENTIAL OF THE HUMAN BEING

Nothing in quantum physics explains what actually happens when a quantum system collapses: does the collapse correspond to a change in the state of the system, or simply to a change in our knowledge of that system? Recently some scientists – including Amit Goswami (quantum physicist), Stanislav Grof (research psychotherapist) and Bruce Lipton (biologist) - have begun to explore and deepen our understanding of the human consciousness as a generator of these "collapses". Perhaps what quantum physics is trying to tell us is that the human mind as an observer brings the rest of the universe into existence. If there were no people to observe it, there would be no universe, except in the form of pure possibility. We must entertain the possibility that it is our consciousness that creates reality. Even if you don't want to go that far, we must still deal with the way the mind perceives, interprets and gives meaning to the sensory impressions it receives. In Chapter 3 we will go deeper into the way the mind processes a personal vision of reality filtered by our culture, influenced by the conditioning of our family, our personal experiences, and our paradigms. This is another source of evidence that there is no objective reality that is separate from the existence of an "observer", or at least from that observer's interpretation.

Returning to the speculations of quantum physics, it is true that the concept of consciousness as the creator of reality is far from having been proven beyond doubt, and certainly does not find favor with all theoretical physicists, but what would happen if we set out to pretend it was true, until someone was able to scientifically prove us wrong?
We have said that our paradigms influence the interpretation we make of the world and its manifestations. Let's try to adopt a new paradigm and imagine the possibility that the quantum phenomena can be applied to our minds and our biology. What are the consequences we anticipate for the human being?
The observer's consciousness would take an observed object in its state of pure potential and make it manifest. Nothing in the universe would exist as an object independent of our perception of it. If we accept this, it means that every minute of every day we create our own world.
Compared to the deterministic view of the world, which has dominated for centuries, the Quantum vision offers incredible possibilities to humankind. It means that we manifest free will in every moment, and that what happens in the future is not necessarily predetermined by the initial conditions. This means that we have great power, the power to change ourselves, our context and our world.
This way of looking at things would invite and encourage a sense of greater personal responsibility, very different from the victim attitude that determinism has invited us to adopt: I'm separated from everyone and everything and I have no power to change my circumstances; if I cannot change anything because everything is already determined by processes that have been set in motion in the past, I cannot help but be subject to the law of cause and effect; nothing that happens is

my responsibility. Liberated from this attitude, we would feel more able to create the conditions for personal evolution and for the evolution of humanity.

Another consequence, if we were to adopt this paradigm, is that we would know we are all made of the same basic materials. At the most fundamental level, all living beings, including humans, would be "quantum energy packets" that exchange information constantly with the endless sea of energy that surrounds them. Everything would be connected with every other thing through an invisible network, and yet local agents like you and me could still control our environment.

I am convinced that there is a pattern at the fundamental level of reality that binds everything together. And these links do not force and compel our local world, but support and release it.

Seen in that light, the "other" is no different from us. We would be able to understand and accept each other at a deeper level if we recognized our sameness. We would avoid many conflicts and wars, we would work together more cooperatively. We would also be more aware of our impact on the environment.

Finally, science and religion could go hand in hand in search of man's ultimate truth because they would not be in opposition anymore. Determinism is no longer suitable for the human being we are becoming. We are developing a new approach free from the chains of separation, free from the lack of purpose and the struggle for survival that has constricted us for four hundred years. The holistic view and the interrelationship of all things are concepts dear to religions and spiritual traditions. Instead of seeing in physics a support for our existing religious beliefs, however, we should use

these findings as an inspiration to rebuild our spiritual ideas.
Quantum mechanics generates a total change of perspective, as Newton's discoveries did a few centuries ago. It's up to us to choose whether to change perspective and see where all this will lead our spiritual thinking. Maybe its emphasis on interconnection could encourage a greater focus on the needs of others and of the environment compared with the paradigm we have accepted up to now. We could also explore the holistic universe as a model of divinity. Maybe the universe is pure consciousness.

COACHING QUESTIONS

What is the paradigm that has governed your life so far?

____

____

____

What could prevent you from having an open mind toward a different view of the world and the way it works?

____

____

____

What or who is the observer?

____

____

____

If the observer creates his own reality, what do you focus your observation on every day? What are you actually creating with the way you observe?

____

____

____

What is the impact of knowing that we create all things, consciously or not?

____

____

____

Part II: Know Thyself

2. Who Am I?

THE VOICE IN MY HEAD

Have you ever noticed that in every moment of your life you have a voice in your head that talks, judges, ruminates? Try to listen to this voice and to experience it now. If at this moment you're telling yourself "What's the voice she's talking about? I don't have any voice in my head"… then that's the voice I mean.

> *What can I write now? Find an example of your own, perhaps. Talk about when you wake up early in the morning with the voice that goes over all the things you need to do during the day. Pretty silly, this is not an interesting example.*

This is the dialogue that is going on at this precise moment in my mind. Can you hear your voice? If you notice, it is always active, jumping from one topic to another, and is sometimes fun. But most of the time it says unnecessary things.

2. Who Am I?

I forgot to buy cat food, maybe I can get closer to that black cat that I have seen in the garden these past few days. The one who looks like Flake, who has been missing for two years. Maybe this one's a bit dumpier than Flake. And the expired mozzarella in the fridge? When do I decide to throw it?

Very often the voice begins to make conjectures and hypotheses on the future that are completely false and based on no objective data. Imagine a sunny day, a beautiful September Sunday, while you're waiting for your boyfriend. You have an appointment at 10 am to go for a walk at the lake and you can already imagine, the sun warming you up as you walk hand in hand and listen to the water lapping on the shore. 10 am comes and he's not there. You call him and nobody answers his cell phone.

Did he say 10 or 11? No, I'm sure he said 10. That's funny, he's a guy who warns you if he's going to be late. Perhaps he's busy on the home phone and can't call me. Who would be so important to hold him on the phone when he should be here? Maybe it's that viper of an ex-girlfriend; I know she's still interested in him. She's around everywhere we go. All those times he answers the phone and talks so cryptically ... I'm sure it's about her. When he arrives I'll show him. Does he think I'm a fool?

And just as he arrives, apologizing for the delay because he could not find a parking space, we are full of explosive energy that detonates to his utter bafflement. And we are capable of ruining our day with senseless discussions that we feed with the excessive emotional charge that builds inside us as a result of the voice. What would you think if a consultant suggested you what your voice did, to scold him? Would you hire him? You wouldn't, would you? Instead you're willing to follow the stupid suggestions of your voice without questioning it. Sometimes, of course, the voice can facilitate your life, but when emotions are involved, then it is able to create quite a mess. Take some time to notice this voice. The voice never stops talking. Sometimes it is so loud that it leaves you sleepless or wakes you up in the middle of the night and does not allow you to go back to sleep. The voice is capable of strongly affirming one thing and a moment later sustaining the exact opposite. One of my coachees named his voice "ribollita", after the famous Tuscan soup that boils for hours. Doesn't it irritate you tremendously? Don't you want to say "Enough is enough, now stop and let me rest"? Of course you cannot shut it up like that, the voice is very persistent.

Why does this voice speak incessantly? There are different reasons that trigger it. One of them is a state of inner imbalance, due to an accumulation of emotions such as anger, fear, anxiety, jealousy, insecurity, worry. The energy that these emotions pump into your body is released through the activity of the voice. At times the voice speaks because she remembers what you've been told in the early years of your life about what you should or shouldn't do to deserve love and attention.

"You must tidy your desk" or "don't go out in the cold without warm clothing". In your childhood all these opinions, reprimands and pieces of advice formed a powerful conditioning. At the time, as we shall see later, your brain did not have the ability to consider and discern if what you were told was relevant or correct. Every judgment or reproach or request was heard as absolute truth. Even today, under certain circumstances, the voice reminds you of what you must and must not do because it believes this will enable you to avoid a punishment or win love and attention.

At other times of your life, however, the voice tells you the experiences you are going through, making you pay attention to some things rather than others. You walk down the road and you see trees, flowerbeds, shops, a passing dog and the voice says: "How green these trees are, they look like trees in the woods on a spring morning. Allowing stores to put ugly-looking signs in such a bucolic landscape ruins everything. The municipal authorities should have a veto power over horrendous signs and shop windows."

This activity seems particularly pointless because you're already living those experiences and you do not need anyone to tell you what you're watching. In reality, the voice makes the things you see and the way you feel about them easier to deal with and more controllable. While narrating the world around you, the experiences you live are brought into the domain of your thoughts and are mixed with all the other streams of thought that you have generated in your life, including thoughts which are the basis of your values. This mix profoundly alters the experience of reality. It is here that we begin to mix events with our judgments and our interpretations, creating a very personal model of meaning-making.

What is outside your body has its own set of rules and variables that are out of your control. When you think, however, you can imagine anything and manipulate your thoughts accordingly. The two streams of information (the perception and the narrative of perception) go hand in hand, in a

mixture that influences your mental construction of the world.
What you capture of what is outside of you passes through a "filter" (formed by past experiences, learned strategies for managing such experiences, paradigms derived from culture, from the family, from the context in which you grew up, etc...) and what arrives in your consciousness is not the reality itself, but your mental model of reality. The mind does a very good job in this regard. It manages your current experiences aligning them with those of the past and the expectations for the future, giving you a feeling of more control. The purpose of this is to allow you to feel you can manage events, because you can manipulate and control your thoughts even if you cannot manipulate or control reality. The price of this process is to live in the mind, instead of being fully present to what is happening.

JOURNEY TO THE CENTER OF CONSCIOUNESS

When I talk about personal transformation, many are assailed by the fear of losing themselves, or at least the person who they believe themselves to be. They identify with their status, their profession, their needs, their emotions, their behaviors, their personality. The idea of transforming one of these elements frightens them. "I would not be myself" they say. Reflecting on "who am I" then, can help to change perspective and to overcome the fear of transformation. Begin with asking yourself: "Who am I?" Ponder this question. What would follow from this thought? You are not your name. The name is a label that conventionally we give ourselves to distinguish ourselves from each other. You're not even your profession because it would

mean that at other times of your life - when you were a student, if you change job or when you retire – you are no longer you, don't you think?
The drama of many managers and business owners today is that they are so identified with their profession and their status that they are not able to find an identity when they lose their job or the privileges of a certain position. I have worked with many top managers and CEOs who were unable to make those changes in life that they really wanted because they could not recognize themselves in another role or with reduced income. It's as if what you are and what you're worth are dependent on the label that your profession gives you. Many people build a cage - often a golden one - in which they perpetuate *ad infinitum* a story of self that does not bring satisfaction or joy, as demonstrated by the development of diseases related to pressure, diseases of the heart, the circulation, or the digestion. Your identity, however, is not your profession, or the task you are carrying out at this particular moment.
Perhaps you begin to understand how deep this questioning of who you are can be. You're not even the body reflected in the mirror because the body and the face you see are completely different at different moments of your life. Who is the person you saw in the mirror twenty years ago and who is that person today? That's right, you're always the one who sees, in a continuity of being. It's you who sees and experiences the objects outside of you. You look and you experience objects inside of you as well, if we can describe as objects the thoughts you have and the emotions you feel, though in this case, since you are the subject, you cannot be the object as well. But in fact you are none of the objects, either outside or inside of you, that constantly demand your attention.

So you're not your profession, your gym card or the role of husband or parent that you carry out. And you're not your emotions or your thoughts, and you are not the voice in your head. All the internal and external objects come and go and they are only entities of which you are aware. Who are you? Who's the one who has these experiences and is aware of these objects?

If you continue to reflect on the question you will notice that you have a special quality. Your quality is consciousness, the awareness that you exist. And you exist with or without certain thoughts, with or without certain memories, with or without labels. There are diseases that deprive us of some parts of our body, but without the use of arms and legs there is still the awareness of existence. There are traumatic brain injuries that do not allow us to remember our past, but still, even in this case, there is the awareness of existing. Consciousness is pure awareness.

•••

"What a liberation to realize that the "voice in my head" is not who I am. Who am I then? The one who sees all this."

Eckhart Tolle

•••

Go back to notice the voice in your head. Don't worry about what it says or how it does it, simply notice it. Listen to it speaking. Whatever it may say, it is only a voice inside your head. You are the one who listens and who notices. The voice is not you, for the simple reason that you are the one who is listening. If you hear something, it's not you, just as if you see something, it's not you. You are the observer. The realization that you are not the voice of the mind, but simply the one who listens, is often the first step toward a personal transformation.

Personal transformation begins by recognizing those parts of us that are afraid and that need to be

protected. One way to do this is to keep reminding yourself that you are the one who listens to the voice talking, but you're not the voice. Then, deepening the understanding of this "observer" and learning how to access this state more often.
Whenever we have a problem we try to solve it by changing what is outside of us, and this rarely works. Sooner or later we meet the same problem again, as if we were in a sort of wheel of fortune that always moves in the same circle. The solution lies in identifying which part of you sees the experience as a problem. To do this you must create a subject-object relationship, in which you enter your position of observer. Doing this will stop you from becoming part of the problem: you're just the one who observes, who is a witness to something, the object that you see happening. This exercise enables you not to feel lost, not to get sucked in by the problem. It trains you to look inside yourself to find solutions, because the solution is not to change what is outside of you.
In Chapter 9, I will give you some tools to train yourself to stay in a state of reflective action, that is, in a state in which you are able to remain an "observer" even when you act in the world.
To the question "Who are you?" now you can answer that you are the one who sees. You are the observer who, in the position in which he finds himself, looks and is aware of objects, events, thoughts and emotions that run in front of him. Now you're in the center of your consciousness, your true home. This is the center of the Self.

CONSCIOUSNESS AND ITS LEVELS

Consciousness is the state of awareness of the self and the environment and it may include thoughts, feelings, emotions, moods and dreams. It is a point of view, it is the knowledge of being deeply "I". It is the essential part of the human being and, incidentally, what has been less well studied by science, because for a long time it has been considered an epiphenomenon - that is, a side effect – of the brain. It is also not as measurable and as predictable as the Newtonian model would require. Materialistic science was more interested in finding out what's out there rather than what is inside us.

Over the past two decades studies in neuroscience have come a long way, because the development of new techniques to observe the brain in terms of structure and function now allow us to bind a specific observed behavior to brain activity.

Recent experiments have shown interesting things. The first is that some aspects of the processes of consciousness can be related to the actions of specific areas of the brain, which open up to the possibility of discovering the neural architecture that supports consciousness. The other interesting aspect which has been discovered is that consciousness and emotions are inseparable.

One of the best-known models related to various levels of consciousness was developed in the 1940s by the American psychologist Abraham Maslow. In his "hierarchy of needs", which you probably know because it has been widely used in pedagogy and in the study of adult learning, Maslow suggests that the lower levels of physical need must be satisfied, before one can move to the higher levels of satisfaction and personal fulfillment. In essence, our primary need as human being is physical survival. Only when this is assured, then we focus on our safety. Then when we feel safe, we shift the focus of our awareness to creating and maintaining relationships that make us feel loved and included in a group.

Figure 2-1: Maslow's Hierarchy of Needs

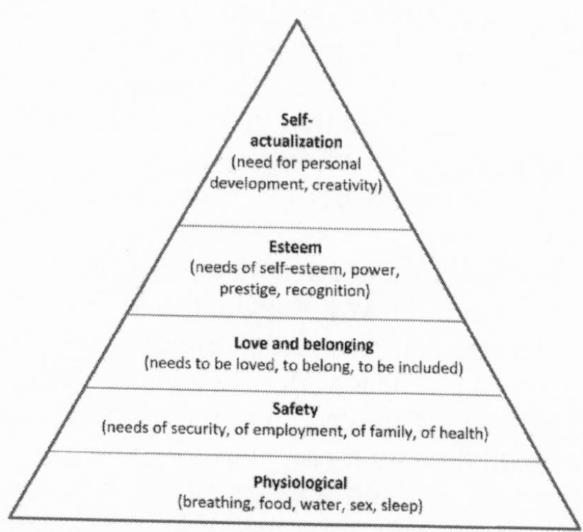

When we have built these relationships, we shift our focus to the need for self-esteem and recognition.

When we comprehend the sense of our self-worth, we focus on self-realization, overcoming the fears that have prevented us from being independent adults.

Many have used and extended Maslow's model in subsequent years. Among them, in the nineties, Richard Barrett took Maslow's hierarchy and shaped the Seven Levels of Consciousness model. According to Barrett, Maslow's categories of needs reflect different states of consciousness. The

Figure 2-23 Barrett's levels of consciousness

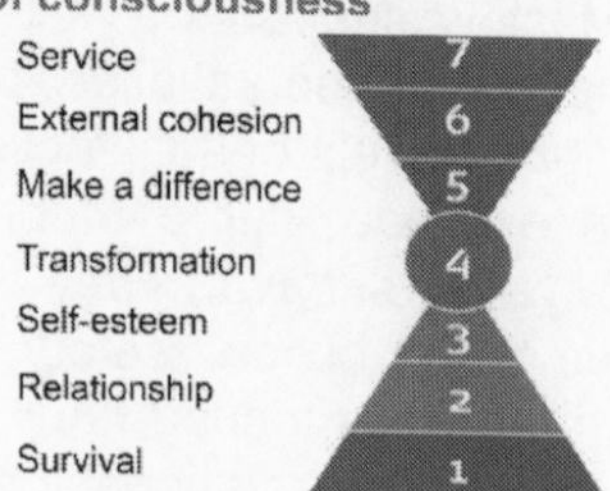

physical and safety needs therefore underlie the level of consciousness called "Survival", followed by the levels of "Relationship" (equivalent of Maslow's social needs) and "Self-esteem" (which corresponds to the affirming needs of the Self). The state that Maslow names Self-realization is expanded by Barrett to include four distinct states in the development of spiritual consciousness: they are the "Transformation", "Internal Cohesion", "Make a Difference" and "Service" levels. With these seven levels of consciousness, Barrett aims to explain the key elements of human interactions.
From a psychological point of view, the first three stages represent the emergence and development of the human Ego. In the presence of unmet needs the individual is guided in life by conscious or subconscious feelings of fear. The last three stages represent the emergence and development (or blossoming) of the human Soul.
Between the last level of development of the Ego and the first level of Soul development there is the level of "Transformation." This is the level at which the person releases the conscious and subconscious fears of the Ego and can reconnect with their Soul (see Figure 2.3).
The motivating forces which correspond to the first three stages are:

- Physical survival: to satisfy basic physiological needs of the person so that they can survive
- Relationship: to meet the emotional and belonging needs of the person so that they can feel safe and protected
- Self-esteem: to satisfy the emotional needs of respect so that the person can feel self-worth

From the perspective of the Ego, all three of these needs are based on dependencies. We satisfy them by trying to get what we want from the outside world.

Figure 2-3 Values associated to Barrett's levels of consciousness

Consciousness levels	Associated values
Level 7: Service	Wisdom, compassion, forgiveness. This is the highest level of internal and external connection and is focused on the service to others. Those who operate from this level are at ease with uncertainty. They are concerned about issues such as social justice, human rights and future generations.
Level 6: Make a difference	Counseling, social commitment, empathy, environmental awareness. This level has to do with making a difference in the world, and the people who operate from this level honor intuition and contribution.
Level 5: Internal Cohesion	Commitment, creativity, enthusiasm, fun, generosity, honesty. This level has to do with a search for meaning.
Level 4: Transformation	Courage, responsibility, continuous learning, independence. This is the level at which people start to overcome their fears. It requires continuous questioning of beliefs and paradigms.
Level 3: Self-esteem	A drive to be the best, ambition, professional growth. The limiting aspects of this level are generated by fears related to low self-esteem and loss of control. The potentially limiting values are status, arrogance, image.
Level 2: Relationship	Friendship, family, respect, open communication. The limiting aspects of this level are generated by fears relating to loss of control or consideration. The potentially limiting values are rivalry, intolerance, a need to be liked.
Level 1: Survival	Financial stability, health, safety, self-discipline, wellness. The limiting aspects of this level are generated by fears related to survival. The potentially limiting values are control, greed, caution.

There are no potentially limiting values on the levels 4 to 7.

The motivating forces that correspond to the three stages in the development of the human Soul are:

- Internal Cohesion: finding personal meaning in life by discovering and integrating the motivations of the Soul
- Make a Difference: acting on the motivations of the Soul and making a difference in the lives of other people or in the community through the expression of our own unique abilities
- Service: when making a difference becomes a permanent way of life we embark on a path of serving others beyond our Ego.

People do not operate from only one of the levels of consciousness, but tend to cluster around three or four levels. There is commonly a distribution between levels 1 and 5.

For example, when a manager at work is extremely competitive, devoting himself entirely to the work, forgetting his family and his hobbies, and is obsessed with demonstrating his skills, he probably has an excess of values in Level 3 and his behavior is based on the fear of losing esteem or of not being worthy of it.

ALIGNING THE NEEDS OF THE EGO AND THE SOUL

As long as the needs of the Ego remain unmet, the Ego cannot fully align with the motivations of the Soul.

To learn how to align the needs of the Ego with those of the Soul is a process that is called "personal transformation" (Level 4), which includes the release of the fears of not having enough, not feeling safe, not feeling worthy. One of the most frequent conflicts between Ego and Soul that people face has to do with work. It is the conflict between survival and self-esteem on one hand and finding meaning and making a difference on the other.

Many people, through various circumstances, find themselves in jobs or careers that offer a good lifestyle, but are meaningless. They do not find passion in the work and look forward to retirement. Without being aware of it, they have chosen the gratification of the Ego instead of that of the Soul. Very often they become aware they are in the wrong job when they have significant financial commitments, such as loans or mortgages to be paid.

The thought of leaving the careers they have chosen to do something they are passionate about makes them too afraid to consider a change. They believe they would have to sacrifice their standard of living to do what they love. The process of resolving these fears is called personal transformation.

When I happen to work with the leaders of large companies and we think about what holds back creativity, performance and a proactive attitude among their employees, these leaders understand that their micromanagement, control, punishment and mistrust (caused by their Ego needs of self-esteem and safety) have created an environment where people are not accountable, do not risk making mistakes and have no space for the creative experience. For this reason, courses and seminars on emotional intelligence or on effective people management have become very fashionable.

The result of many of these courses, however, is only a rational understanding of the issue, since they do not offer the path required to support leaders in transcending their fears and seeing themselves in a completely different relationship with employees, free from basic Ego needs. For this to happen, we need a personal transformation. Personal transformation is never bound to a single event. It is a continuous meeting between the needs generated by the subconscious fear-based beliefs and the needs of the Soul. At every meeting we have to learn how to put together the needs of the Ego and those of the Soul. While the Ego is tough, dominant and wants to control, the Soul is soft, patient, flexible and yearns for meaning and connection.

A Level 3 Issue

In a big, well-known multinational company, the vast majority of managers who did a personality assessment share the same profile, the one defined "insecure overachiever". In this company, managers are always under pressure for results, are asked to follow projects in different parts of the world and to travel seamlessly. Very often the managers meet their families only on weekends, they must always be available for their clients and they keep working even when they could rest. Of course, the company is not responsible for making them "insecure overachievers". The values of competition, success and image that the firm presents to the world attract people who can find in that context a good gym to demonstrate their worth and to exorcize the fear of lack of self-esteem.

In this case, both the company and the managers have a reciprocal interest to attract one another. Each of them satisfies the needs of the other. Over the last few years, however, this company has been facing a leadership issue. The current leaders are not role models and inspiration for the younger talents and this generates an extremely high turnover. Young professionals stay two or three years to "build their curriculum" and then leave. Many young managers, notwithstanding their desire for a well-paid and prestigious job, are not ready to see their profession and their success as the only components of their lives. They have a more holistic view, and work is just one of the many expressions of their existence. For them their job must have meaning and not be a compensation to their fears.

Regular emotional upsets or bursts of anger are warning signs that the Ego is not in alignment with the Soul and is still dealing with unresolved fear-based beliefs. The person has to deal with herself and overcome the fears of the Ego. The process of realignment with the Soul is often painful, requiring courage and a willingness to work on the sufferings of the past which are the basis of the fear-based beliefs. These sufferings are memories that originate in a state of unresolved need for internal stability and external balance that we experienced in the formative years of our life[3].

FROM CONSCIOUSNESS TO EGO

To better understand the roles of the Ego and the Soul and their continuous process of alignment – which happens whether we are conscious of it or not, and especially in the Western world where the Ego needs too often prevail - we can use the transpersonal approach to human development. Transpersonal psychology is the study of the higher potential of the human being and includes the understanding and realization of the spiritual and transcendent states of consciousness. Roberto Assagioli (1888-1974), theosophist and psychiatrist with a transpersonal approach, proposed a model that can help us understand the connection

[3] The copyright on the Seven Levels of Consciousness is Richard Barrett's. On www.valuescentre.com/pva you can find a self-assessment to learn what levels your consciousness operates at.

between the Ego and the Transpersonal Self (the term that Assagioli used to define the Higher Self or Soul). According to this scholar, the center of the Self, or the Personal Self, is the essence of the person and has the two functions of consciousness (or awareness) and will. The Personal Self is dynamic and receptive: it has the ability to reflect both on the content of consciousness and on consciousness itself. It does this by choosing to focus awareness (as occurs in many types of meditation) and to expand or contract it.

The Ego, or field of active and thinking consciousness, is that part of our psyche that is thinking, speaking, reading, and remembering right now. It is that part of the mind with which you express your individuality and that gives you the sense of "I" and "mine." It is the expression of your personality. Whenever you think, speak or do something, you put the Ego into play. The experiences of shame, fear, grief, despair and anger associated with the wounds suffered in the primitive stage of your life, and all the unrecognized fear-based beliefs are relegated to the Lower Unconscious.

Figure 2-4 Assagioli's Model of the Person

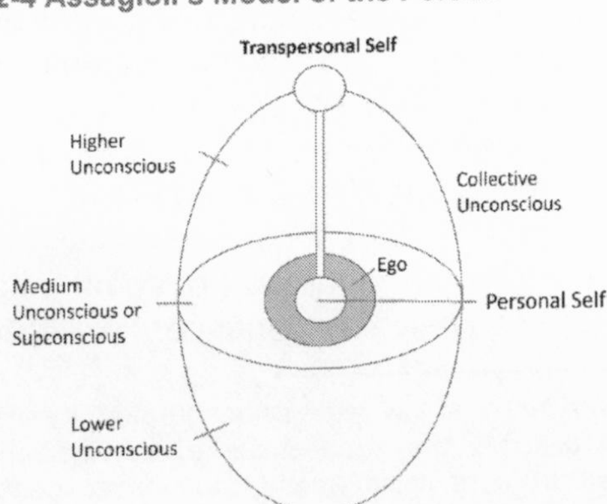

The Subconscious or Medium Unconscious, easily accessible with a voluntary recall to consciousness, represents the space where daily experiences are processed and streamlined.
Here we use our sense of discernment and judgment, we develop attitudes and apply reasoning skills. This level contains only what we are prepared to accept in our reality. The insights, ideas, inspirations, moral and ethical impulses, the states of enlightenment and contemplation, premonitions and experiences of ecstasy come from the Higher Unconscious.
Finally, in Assagioli's model we find the Transpersonal Self, which pervades all areas of the diagram and is connected with them all. The Transpersonal Self is a source of wisdom and guidance, which can operate without the direct control of the conscious mind. Continuous alignment with the Higher Self can bring the person to every place in the diagram, depending on the individual direction. It can for example lead to the high point of spiritual and creative experiences (peak experience[4]), to a sense of unification with the whole, to re-experience the wounds of early childhood or to discern a sense of purpose and meaning in life.
The Ego, in short, is the protagonist of our present mental plane. There are some exceptions, for example when we are so absorbed in an artistic activity or in listening to beautiful music that we feel pretty much lost or, as they say, "in the flow". In this case the sense of the "I" is attenuated or even temporarily stopped. Similarly in some religious, spiritual or meditative experiences we lose our

---

[4] *Peak experience* is an expression created by Abraham Maslow to describe the experiences of transpersonal and ecstatic nature, in particular those experiences denoted by harmonization and interconnection, with a spiritual quality.

sense of individuality and feel almost fused with the object of contemplation. But apart from these exceptional circumstances, the Ego is always with us. It is a wire that connects all the different parts of individuality and gives them cohesion.
The Ego, however, needs to identify with something, otherwise it cannot express itself. This is why every time we say: "I am a professional", "I'm hungry", "I am sad" and so on, our mind creates the illusion of identification with objects, thoughts or emotions. In the transpersonal approach, the human being is seen as incomplete, pursuing self-realization along an existential and spiritual path that is essentially endless.
The Transpersonal Self is the realm of the Soul. At this level our Soul knows everything about the life we are leading, it knows what it hopes to achieve and why it chose some particular circumstances for its experience. Our ability to "tune" in to the transpersonal Self allows us access to our wisest part, which may indicate to us the path toward our complete realization as human beings.
Certain events occurred in our lives because the Soul chose them as learning experiences for our personality. It's as if something, deep within us, attracted to us certain circumstances, to give us the opportunity to grow and evolve.
It's up to us to recognize these circumstances as an opportunity and to choose to use them to grow, instead of seeing them as obstacles or hassles which we feel victims of. In Chapter 8, I will offer you an exercise to use upsetting events as a springboard toward personal transformation.
If we train ourselves to shift the focus of our awareness from the Ego to the Personal Self we gain access to higher levels of consciousness up to the Transpersonal Self. As the quantum mechanics seems to suggest, in higher states of

consciousness every possibility coexists as a field of energy, which "collapses" into form and matter to manifest itself in the three-dimensional world.
It is the conscious observer who, through the thoughts, emotions and beliefs that constitute their awareness, chooses from among all the as yet unmanifested possibilities to create the form that reality will take.
But we cannot venture into the realm of the Personal Self if we do not understand and experience how the Ego works and how it can limit our potential.

THE NATURE OF OUR BEHAVIOR

It is important to get a better understanding of what are the drivers of our behavior, so that we will then be able to transform them. To do this, you can begin to familiarize yourself with the iceberg model. In this model, the part of us that is visible to others - and sometimes even to ourselves, unfortunately - is relatively small.
In Figure 2.5 you can see that the emerged part of the iceberg and the other levels are separated by the water line. The line separates what is observable by others from what is not. Such evaluation can be subjective, of course, and in that case it will not be without personal prejudices. Let me give an example.
I grew up in a Mediterranean culture, where we express ourselves in a loud tone of voice, where we laugh out loud, where the words are often underlined by a lot of gestures and energy. In my family, it is absolutely normal to be open and noisy. If I meet a potential customer living in Val D'Aosta - whose culture is reserved and where movements are contained - what he can observe without any doubt is that I make sweeping movements with my

arms when I speak, I use a tone of voice louder than average and I am very direct. All this is observable.

Less observable are the thoughts or emotions that underlie my behavior. My prospective client from Val d'Aosta can only make some guesses, but they will be affected by the paradigm and culture of that region. While I may feel excited and think that having a new customer in Val D'Aosta could open doors to more business in a region where I have not previously established my company, he could have the perception that I am aggressive and trying to dominate our communication.

The difference between what is visible and what is not is important because very often we expect others to be able to understand what we think or feel, as if they had a crystal ball. If we do not open up and make our thoughts and our emotions manifest, we leave the field open to assumptions (and these rarely turn out to be correct).

Figure 2-5 The Iceberg Model

Below the water line, in the non-visible part, we first find thoughts and emotions. What we think and feel has a strong influence on our behavior. Let's imagine you're at the coffee shop for a cappuccino. You've just signed a contract with a company for a new project and the CEO complimented you on your creativity and professionalism.

Your self-esteem needs are met and there is also a beautiful sunlight here in this lovely square in downtown Milan. Here comes the waiter who stumbles and pours some cappuccino over you. He turns to you with a contrite apology; he says he is desperately sorry. Your heart is still full of joy and satisfaction even if you were surprised when you saw the cup falter, and the thought that comes to your head is "Why bother about this little incident?" You say to the waiter "Don't worry, it happens. Would you bring some stain remover, please?"

Imagine the same scene, the same coffee shop, the only difference is that this time you are back from a meeting at which the customer did not show up. He sent an unpleasant and spiteful junior assistant who got critical about the project, and queried every single detail. He reminded you of the way your professor got on your nerves when he highlighted all your shortcomings. The meeting dragged on for two hours and you seem to have lost the contract. You have also just lost your mobile phone complete with your electronic diary and you did not do any back up recently. You tried to take a taxi back to the office because you had an appointment half an hour later, but Milan is blocked due to the Fashion Fair and there are no taxis available. Let me imagine how you would react to the waiter who pours the cappuccino over you – more aggressively, perhaps: "No excuses, you're utterly incompetent, you don't even know how to hold a cup. I'll have these clothes cleaned and I expect you to pay the bill!"

Underneath our thoughts and emotions, there is another level where our values and our priorities reside, which affects our thoughts and emotions. Imagine that one of your values is respect for others. Imagine that this is a foundation element of your value system. Every human being has the right to be treated with dignity, respect and courtesy, especially if he is in a condition apparently subordinate to yours. It was taught to you by your family. In your house, for example, the cleaning lady had an important role and you never heard your mother or your father disrespecting her, never heard her insulted or belittled. Once you were rude to her and you were punished. You've had a series of experiences that have reinforced this value of yours. And you made it a priority always to choose environments where human talent is recognized and people treated with dignity. This value would support your kind answer to the waiter's apology.

Imagine instead that one of your values is perfection. You are happy when you accomplish a task flawlessly, you like accuracy and completeness. You have high expectations of yourself and others. You cannot stand it when people don't take their work seriously or do it in a superficial way. You are convinced that the world is full of people who are not seeking the level of quality that you yearn for in everything you do. You care more about results than relationships. This value of perfection could generate an irritable answer to the waiter because his behavior (not paying enough attention to where he's walking and risking accidents) triggers this value, pressing one of your buttons.

When working with managers, I find that one of the typical behaviors that prevents them from bringing out the best in the people they lead is wanting to

control everything, which results in an enormous waste of time and energy (of the manager and of his co-workers), and the task is still not perfect as it would have been if they had personally performed it (does this sound familiar?).
This need for continuous monitoring could emerge from a value of perfection. Instead of risking what he would perceive as a mistake or failure, the manager puts under pressure - and attempts to control - the people who work alongside him, limiting their creativity and their own willingness to take risks.

NEEDS GUIDE OUR BEHAVIOR

The impulses of the Transpersonal Self toward self-realization inspire our behaviors, but these impulses are too often overwhelmed by the fear of not meeting a particular need and by the mechanisms of protection that the Ego practices.
What unleashes our fears are our unmet needs. Needs create filters with which we color the way we see and understand ourselves, the world, the events and circumstances around us. And our needs generate the values, which in turn give rise to the way we think and feel, which in turn will generate our behaviors. From the bottom of the iceberg a series of consequences in the way we interpret and respond to the world are triggered. And from the bottom of the iceberg stem our paradigms. All of us are born completely vulnerable and unable to be independent. We are not able to find our own food or protect ourselves from harm. Our survival is completely in the hands of our parents or those who take care of us. Since birth, in addition to the physiological needs of being fed and cared for in our basic functions, we have a range of psychological needs that must be met so that we

can live and grow in a healthy way. These needs come in polarities[5]: one need is at one pole and the other at the opposite pole. On one hand there is the need for love and belonging: the child must feel the unconditional love of the parents or caretakers, as well as their recognition and acceptance. On the other hand there is the need for self-expression, to make autonomous choices as an independent being.

Another polarity involves the need for safety. The child must feel physically and psychologically safe. The way in which safety is experienced is through predictability. A safe environment is one in which the child has the perception that he will be fed and his mother will be there in case of danger not only today, but also tomorrow and in the future. However, if the environment is always and constantly safe and predictable, it gives little stimulus to the child's growth and learning. So at the other pole there is the need for variety and unpredictability. We can observe this pair of opposite needs when we see a child who stays close to the mother but who at some point leaves the safety to explore new territories.

In his early months and years, the child's only concern is to satisfy these four needs (love, self-expression, predictability and variety) and he is physiologically equipped from his birth to monitor the environment in order to identify what would meet his needs or keep his needs unmet. He does this through the reptilian brain, the first stage of development of the brain. We will later understand how the brain activates an ingenious safeguard

5 The idea of the polarities of needs in the iceberg model has been formulated by the coach and great friend Nadjeschda Taranzcewski.

mechanism against dangers in a completely automatic way.
There are also two other needs, constituting an innate tension in every human being, that we call "soul needs", because they are not related to our Ego but rather to our Transpersonal Self: the need for personal growth and the need for contribution.
The presence of needs is functional to an individual's development since they provide the impetus to act, to satisfy the need and avoid what is dangerous. We can notice the same mechanism (attraction to pleasure and away from danger) also in the individual cells of our body. When researchers remove cells from our bodies and make them grow in specific cultures, the cells actively search for those environments that support their survival and at the same time "avoid" hostile or toxic ones. Each single-celled organism has the equipment to analyze thousands of external stimuli and select appropriate behavioral responses to ensure their survival.
When these needs are met – during childhood by parents, relatives or others in support roles such as "nannies", in subsequent years by teachers and classmates, and in adult life by people themselves - then the development of the psyche has no limit. If instead one of the needs is at an early stage totally or partially denied, the subconscious creates a whole series of protections and develops fear. This fear will color all the overlying layers of functioning, and will affect relationships. When the child does not get the four elements that he needs to survive - love, safety, variety and self-expression – he perceives danger and reacts immediately. He is not able to contain his emotions, to "be" with them and assess whether the external elements represent a real danger to him, but is immediately reactive.

When these dangers are experienced in a very strong or prolonged way the child, who has not yet developed the more advanced features of the rational mind, stores all the sensations associated with those dangers in his body and nervous system in an unconscious way - as the sense of self or self-consciousness develops only much later - and develops a deep unmet need that will be relived as an adult in an equally powerful way as soon as a precipitating cause presents itself.

The child grows into his adulthood, taking with him a wealth of needs. Some support his advancement in life, because they constitute a powerful motivation. Others, that were satisfied in a conditional way or have been denied, are those unmet needs that often remain in the unconscious domain, and that manifest themselves through a dysfunctional behavior.

In the culture of my family children were not allowed to express their dissent or to challenge the beliefs of adults. I was the youngest, and anyone, compared to me, was an adult. So I could not express my opposition, or more simply what I believed, when it was different from what the adults thought.

This lack of freedom of speech has profoundly affected me and remained entangled in my neurological system as a warning sign of grave danger. One of the values that I have developed is "full expression" of myself and others. It is so important to me that in the past I felt anger and impatience, and developed attitudes of protection that were triggered whenever I sensed that people around me, especially those in positions of authority, were not listening to me or were preventing me from voicing my opinions.

At that time I already held a leadership position, and I experienced the disruptive effect of this mechanism when I had a boss whom I experienced as dominating and unwilling to listen to my reasoning. After some early misunderstandings, he began to make demands on me and impose tasks that I did not agree with, and he refused to listen to my point of view. I found it hard to contain the feeling of anger, or hold myself back from behaving aggressively and challenging him, my reactive way of protecting myself. In turn, my manner made him even more imposing and directive.

There's no need to explain how these initial misunderstandings escalated to become a real conflict, which knocked me flat, both physically and psychologically. If I had had the awareness I have now, if I had used the Practice of the Four S that you will learn in Chapter 8, I would have recognized that the experience of intimidation was due to my hypersensitivity, which arose from my needs and my system of paradigms, and that it was possible to see the same chain of events in a completely different way. I then would have had the opportunity to choose the most functional behavior to adopt to achieve my true objectives (finding satisfaction in work, feeling I had an important role in the success of the company). Instead, at the time I was sucked in by the reactions of my Ego to the danger that my needs were being disregarded, and I was not able to handle the situation in a conscious and constructive way.

EXERCISE: BUILD YOUR ICEBERG

I invite you now to build your iceberg and find out what might be the mechanisms that trigger a dysfunctional or self-sabotaging behavior, preventing you from reaching what you really want.

Start by identifying one or two behaviors ("what I do" or "what I say") that you believe hinder the growth of your career or optimal relationships with others, that is, dysfunctional behaviors (for example: "I am not able to say no to my boss and my colleagues when they ask me to take care of yet another project and I load myself with too much work"):

____

____

____

Let's begin to explore the part that is not visible from the outside, that is, feelings and thoughts. "What do you think" and "what do you feel" in relation to this behavior? (For example: "I think that helping others is a generous offer, but it becomes a double edged sword if I cannot create boundaries. The emotion I feel is frustration because when I accept the zillionth project I put my personal commitments at risk: I know I will postpone my private life in order to be able to finish the job.")

____

____

____

What value or priority in your life seems to support this behavior? (For example: "I was taught and I strongly believe that being helpful to others is an act worthy of great respect and appreciation.")

____

____

____

Now think of your behavior as a way you found, during your life, to protect you from something. How does your behavior protect you? Or ask yourself:

what is the advantage of continuing to enact this behavior? (For example: "Saying yes and accept the work that is given to me by colleagues and the boss allows me to be perceived as a generous, helpful worker, and whom you can rely on.")

____

____

____

Let's take a step further. What is the worst thing that can happen if what you just described, the advantage obtained from continuing to persue that behavior, doesn't come true? What would happen otherwise? (For example: "If they don't perceive me as a generous employee they may think I'm selfish, that I do not devote myself enough to the company.")

____

____

____

Let's try to explore the worst case scenario ... what is the worst thing that could happen if what you have just described came true? What is your real fear? (For example: "if they think I'm selfish and insufficiently committed they will turn away from me. My fear is of being rejected.")

____

____

____

What is the unmet need that underlies this fear? (For example: "The need to be accepted.")

____

____

Were you able to get to the source of the unwanted behavior? This is an exercise that you can repeat whenever you want to understand the need at the basis of a behavior that becomes an obstacle to the achievement of your goals.
Another exercise you can do is to start from an unmet need you know you have carried with you for a long time and "climb" the iceberg to understand what behaviors you are adopting as a protection against your fear.
It is worthwhile to work with a partner who knows you well. Very often what is not clear and visible to us is very obvious to those around us. To facilitate your task of exploration, I suggest below some of our most common needs as human beings, all arising from the main four (love, safety, variety and self-expression). It is not an exhaustive list, but it can help you reflect on your unmet needs:

- *be accepted* (get approval, feel included, be respected, feel empowered, be considered, be encouraged)
- be loved (please others, be esteemed, be treated affectionately, be attractive, be wanted, be preferred)
- *recognition* (receive flattery, be appreciated, be praised, receive compliments, be rewarded, be thanked, be noticed, be remembered, receive honors, be known for…)
- *demonstrate own value* (gain, achieve victory, implement, arrive, reach, make a career, get responsibilities, be industrious, achieve high performance, be perfect)
- *be considered* (get attention, be treated with tenderness, be helped, be heard, feel loved, be taken into consideration)

- *be right* (correct others, be morally right, avoid mistakes, be an example, get validation)
- *order* (order, perfection, sequence, predictability, control, accuracy, consistency)
- *power* (exercise authority, exhibit power, demonstrate skills, demonstrate strength, be influential)
- *safety* (feel fully informed, be cautious, feel protected, weigh things up, stay alert, find stability, feel supported)
- *independence* (free to express oneself, free from tight bonds, self-sufficient)
- *creativity* (have space to create, not have limits, not have to follow rules)
- *variety* (change, unpredictability, out of the routine, receive surprises)

COACHING QUESTIONS

What are your reflections on the needs you have identified?
Have you had any surprises?

____

____

____

At what level of consciousness do you act when your behavior is not functional?

____

____

____

What level of consciousness is the least familiar to you and represents a possible area of development?

____

____

____

What paradigm did you have in mind when you read the section of Assagioli's model of the person? What reactions did you feel? How did you act on them?

____

____

____

3. How Do We Know What We Know

"Know thyself." This aphorism, in ancient Greece, was inscribed on Apollo's Temple in Delphi and refers to the ideal of knowledge of human behavior, of morality, of thought; because developing the understanding of self means understanding others as well. The saying sums up the teaching of Socrates, who exhorted his disciples to find the truth within themselves and not in the world of appearances and illusion.
Thinkers such as Socrates himself and, in the twentieth century, Krishnamurti stressed the fact that the world - which is to be known in a direct and active way - cannot be understood if we do not already understand how our mind works, how it knows and recognizes things. Understanding the mind's functioning means being able to free ourselves from prejudice and cultural conditioning and know without filters.
What we will embark on together in this chapter and the next three (*4. The software with which we are programmed, 5. The intelligence of the heart*

and our emotions, and *6. Our evolutionary path*) will be an attempt to better understand how we learn, how we perceive reality, which neurological and biological mechanisms are the basis of some of our reactions, what function emotions have and how we "feel" them.
Only if we develop a greater awareness of ourselves and our way of "working" will we have the opportunity to transform those behaviors and those paradigms that are not especially useful and choose which impulses shall drive our life: fear or love and desire to fulfill ourselves to the best of our possibility.

PLATO AND THE MYTH OF THE CAVE

Plato, one of the most creative and influential disciples of Socrates, sums up in his work, *The Republic,* his view of an ignorant humanity, trapped and unaware of its own limited perspective, by using the allegory of the cave.

•••
"Reality is merely an illusion, although very persistent.
Albert Einstein
•••

Imagine a group of men who have lived since childhood in a large cavern. They are chained so that they can look only in front of them at a blank wall. The light of a fire, burning behind them, projects shadows on the wall. The shadows are those of people who walk and carry objects along a road that runs between the fire and the chained men. Having no point of comparison and not being able to turn around, these prisoners take the shadows of the objects projected on the wall as reality.
What this allegory tells is that the prisoners in the cave (that is, human beings) do not see reality, but only a representation of it (shadows). At the base of Plato's vision is the belief that there are actually

invisible realities that lie beneath the apparent surface of things, that only the most "enlightened" can grasp. The prisoners are so accustomed to the illusion of the cave that at the beginning they resist the light, just as students resist education.
At the end of this allegory, Plato mentions another of his ideas: education is not a process by which empty minds are filled with knowledge, but it consists in making people aware of what they already know. The notion that truth and knowledge are already integrated in our minds proved to be very powerful and has influenced the culture and education throughout the centuries. Even today this concept inspires the philosophy of coaching[6].

THOUGHTS CREATE REALITY

What can be defined as "real"? The question sounds strange, I know that.
Probably, like the participants in our workshops, you might answer: the house in which I live is real, the tree that I see from the window is real, the fact that as a child I fell down and I wounded my leg, on which I still bear the scar, is real. We look around and see "real" things: chairs, lamps, tables, cars, bricks, televisions, trees... could you say with absolute conviction that these elements are real?
Most people think that something is real when you can see it, touch it, and perceive it with your senses. And science has supported this interpretation for four hundred years: all that is

---

[6] Coaching as a discipline that supports individuals and groups to express their potential and to reach their objectives, is based on a few basic principles. One of these is that the coachee has already everything she needs to reach the results she desires and the coach helps her to access to her resources. The coach does not give suggestions and advice, but helps to expand her consciousness.

perceived by the five senses (or by tools that extend our sensory capacity) is real.

The opposite works as well: what is not perceived by the senses is not real. When you begin to understand how so-called "reality" is absorbed and filtered by our senses you begin to doubt this distinction.

The first to develop a theory of visual perception which claimed that vision occurs in the brain rather than the eye was Ibn al-Haytham (965-1038), an Arabic or Persian Muslim scientist, who contributed greatly to the progress of disciplines such as optics, anatomy, astronomy, medicine, ophthalmology, philosophy and the sciences in general. In 1021 he wrote the *Book of Optics*, in which he argued that personal experience has an impact on what people see and how they see, and that vision is subjective[7]

.

Ibn al-Haytham says, for example, that a person can make a mistake in his vision because his personal experience suggests that what he is seeing is one thing, while in reality it is something different. The police know this mechanism very well: when questioning two witnesses of the same accident, who witnessed the accident from the same position, they often report very different descriptions.

Hermann von Helmholtz (1821-1894) is a German physician who studied visual perception and contributed greatly to the subject in the modern age. His studies on vision describe the eye as a very poor tool – at the optical level - so much so that vision seems impossible. Helmholtz concludes from his research that vision can only be the result of an unconscious inference: this means that our

---

[7] Bradley Steffens (2006), *ibn al.Haytham: First Scientist*, Morgan Reynolds, Greensboro, 2007

visual perception is a process by which we make assumptions and draw conclusions, from incomplete data, on the basis of previous experiences. We only take a small amount of partial information from our senses and then "rebuild" what we see based on our previous experience of that object or other similar ones.

Just to give one very trivial example, I once walked on the beach and I "saw" a big dark stone half stuck in the sand. I took a swim, then I laid in the sun close to that big dark rock, until a few hours later I got closer and touched that "thing", and realized that it was probably a deformed buoy that the sea had brought ashore, and that had sunk in the sand. My mind, of course, had never experienced such a deformed buoy before, so it "saw" what seemed more normal on a beach, where one generally finds stones and rocks in and out of the water: a large dark stone. Hence the need to have a certain experience of the world to give meaning to the input we receive from the senses.

More recent research gives substance to Helmholtz's theory. It seems that the brain processes visual information to construct an image. First of all the brain divides visual stimuli into shapes, colors and basic patterns. Then it starts to combine these vague images with stored memories of similar things, and to associate them with related meanings and emotions, trying to put everything together in an integrated image. Than it "shoots" this image in the frontal lobes forty times per second.

That's right, we don't even see on a continuous basis, but in the form of fast "frames". The brain then "creates" whatever you're seeing by referring to memories of similar things (colors, sizes, shapes, emotions, and meanings) and then putting them all together.

Our perceptual capacities are very limited. We cannot see infrared light, for example, or perceive the magnetic fields as certain birds do. We are not able to process all the information that we receive through the five senses, that is about 400 billion bits per second. Researchers claim that only 2,000 bits come to our awareness. So our brain must discard a lot of information. How does the brain make sense of all this ocean of information it receives in every moment?

Imagine you are in the office preparing a report for your boss. Much of the information you're getting is not relevant for the task you are performing (for example, the temperature of the room, the perception of the chair on which you are seated, the type of light that illuminates the room, the sticky notes with reminders of what you need to do and so on). The brain then inhibits what is already "known" so that you can ignore all the elements that are not useful to you in that moment. By this process certain pieces of neural information are prevented from coming to your consciousness[8].

The study of visual illusions (cases in which the process of inference proves to be wrong) has offered many insights into what kind of deductions our visual system makes. Let me show you some of the visual illusions that I find most fascinating.

What did you see in *Figure 3.1*?

---

[8] Andrew Newberg, Director of Clinical Nuclear Medicine, Director of NeuroPET Research, and Associate Professor of Radiology at the University of Pennsylvania School of Medicine. Cfr. Eugene D'Aquili, Andrew B. Newberg, *The Mystical Mind*, Fortress Press, Minneapolis, 1999.

Figure 3-1 What do you see in the image?

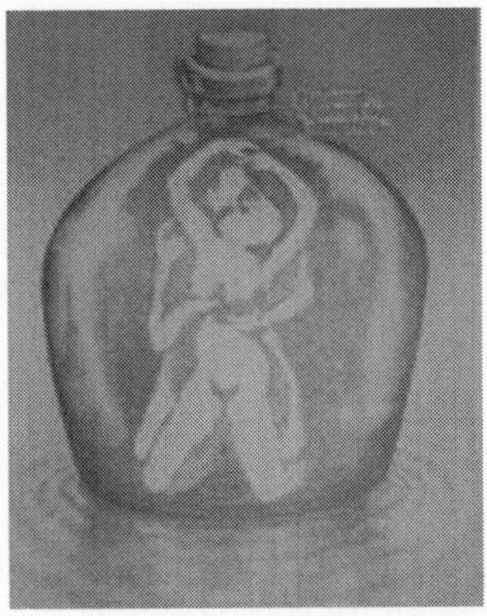

I suspect that you have immediately seen the image of a man and a woman embracing each other in a sensual movement. If this picture was shown to children you'd get a different answer. Children, in fact, who haven't yet integrated the erotic side of human behavior, will probably tell you that they see nine dolphins.

Did you see them too? Go back and look at the picture again.

Now, look at *Figure 3.2*.

Figure 3-2 How many elements do you see?

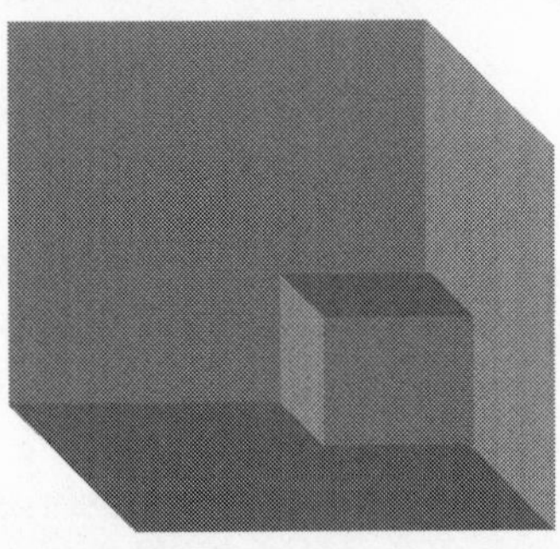

Look carefully for fifteen seconds, then - without reading ahead, don't cheat! - write what you saw:

Now, look again and figure out if you can see something else, an image that was not immediately obvious during the first viewing. When you've found it, write it below:

Finally, go back to the figure again and try to find out what is the third image you can see. What? You don't see anything else? Try again. Do you give up? Then later I'll reveal the three images. For now, focus on completing this chapter.

We do not perceive reality, but we see an image of it that our brain has elaborated on the basis of sensory information, as well as on numerous associations built on past experiences drawn from all its networks. It is the brain that perceives reality and creates our subjective interpretation of it.

Have you ever thought that the idea of an objective reality in which the world is solid and real is maybe a product of social conditioning? There is no proof that the world is real. It is an assumption that has not yet been either proved or disproved. How can you be certain that the world is not a dream?

Experiments in neuroscience have shown that the brain does not know the difference between what it sees and what it thinks. It taps into the network of past experiences and uses them as a model of the present. Research in this field was conducted with scanning equipment - such as positron emission tomography (PET) or positron in single photon emission computed tomography (SPECT) - or with devices for nuclear magnetic resonance imaging (MRI).

In these experiments, people were asked to look at an object, for example a vase. The researchers checked which areas of the brain and which processes were activated, and observed a particular pattern. Then researchers asked participants to close their eyes and imagine or visualize the same vase.

By monitoring the brain at this stage, researchers were able to demonstrate that the same parts of the brain and the same processes would be activated, as if the person was really seeing the object.

These are extraordinary results, showing that thinking and perceiving activate the same brain states, but they also warn us that, for our brains, perceiving a thing or thinking it does not make much difference. The model of the world we have in our mind creates the reality that we see out there. Is the reality, therefore, outside of us, or in our mind? When I open my eyes I do not see "the world", but the interpretation my sensory system and my paradigms allow me to see.

●●●

"Have you ever had a dream, Neo, and been certain that it was true? What would happen if you weren't able to wake up from that dream? How will you know the difference between the dream and the real world?
Morpheus, in The Matri

●●●

Imagine you're at the central station, with thousands of passengers walking and talking, machines making noise, employees preparing sandwiches and drinks. Everything is mixed into a background din. You're not interested in distinguishing any sound or image. Hundreds of thousands of bits of information are entering the field of your consciousness, but only a very small part comes to your conscious mind. At one point there comes an announcement that mentions the destination you're trying to get to.

Immediately your attention goes to the message that seems to emerge from the indistinct sea of sounds. The mechanism that allows us to focus our attention on the part that is relevant to us is called Reticular Activator System (RAS) and it makes sure that we are not overwhelmed by information. The problem is that the RAS filters reality, allowing only a fraction of what is out there to reach our conscious mind. When you change your focus, you change the way in which the Reticular Activating System filters reality.

Have you ever wanted to change your car, and started to get interested in a new model you hadn't commonly seen in the streets? And once you start paying attention to it, you notice a lot of those cars around that you had never noticed before? Or when you have never heard the name of a band and from the moment you focus your attention on it, you begin to hear their songs everywhere or to read about concerts that the band is going to perform? Does this mean that before focusing your attention on the car or the band they did not exist? Certainly they didn't exist in your consciousness, in your experience of the world.

Our awareness of the environment is based on a cycle of feedback in which the data that we receive from the senses are filtered and then transmitted to the central nervous system. This cycle builds our "model of the world." We assimilate it as information at an unconscious level and then we use it to identify beliefs and behaviors, which in turn create new systems.

The models of reality that we create on the basis of our belief systems and our experiences differ from reality because we intervene as we are receiving pieces of information by deleting, distorting or generalizing them so that they can adhere to our model of reality. This in turn depends on the experiences we have had, by how we reacted to these experiences, and by the responses we received from the environment. And since everyone has a different nervous system, we perceive different things and have different experiences. My "reality" is different from your "reality", and it may be either in a subtle, almost imperceptible way, or to a great extent.

Would you perhaps say that the events of the past are as real as you remember them, and that you are confident that they happened in the same way as they show up in your memory? Even the past, in fact, is filtered by the brain and recent studies show that the brain rebuilds the past in a process full of errors of perception, false memories, and judgment. The system works automatically and outside of our awareness. Have you ever tried to compare your memory of a past event with that of a family member or a person that has experienced the same event? You will rarely both remember two identical realities.

Sometimes we have heard stories of certain events so many times that we have included them as part of our reality, while we have no evidence that they occurred. When a statement is repeated often enough, our brain tends to accept it as a fact. This effect is based on familiarity: the more something is repeated, the more familiar it becomes and the more we are inclined to believe that there is some truth in it. Think about the devastating effect that this mechanism creates when children are continually given negative feedback. In the long run they begin to accept that feedback as reality.

OBSERVER-CREATED REALITY

We go around in life with paradigms that become our beliefs and that we never question. The most powerful paradigms are built around our unmet needs in order to protect ourselves from the risk of suffering. These paradigms, namely what we firmly believe, appear to us as "truth", and give shape to the reality we observe.

Let us go back to the example of the person who believes in the value of perfection, who always seeks the best way of doing things. The unmet need that underlies this value is probably to be loved unconditionally. In childhood she learned that to be loved she must become a perfect, good girl, so she continues to behave like that to deserve love. In the office the value of perfection makes life difficult for those who work with her. She does not trust others because she believes that they are not able to do a job as perfectly as she would and she always puts everyone under pressure. Her paradigm is: "Nobody can do it like I do." She deeply believes it. And with this paradigm, with this conviction, she observes reality.

Figure 3-3 Observer-Created Reality

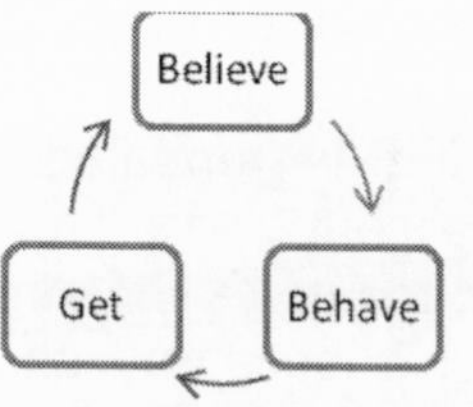

What do you think will happen when her staff shows up? She will make sure that they do exactly what she would have done. She will find mistakes, make negative comments. She will not be able to accept different ideas. They may be innovative but they are different from her own (which are perfect). So she will act with respect to her own paradigms.

By focusing on the mistakes and deficiencies in the work performed by her employees, our protagonist will get exactly what she expected: the work is not as good as hers, and this will only strengthen her

paradigm. Here's how our thoughts become a self-fulfilling prophecy.
In the long term, knowing what they can expect and remembering the feeling of frustration felt when unable to get recognition for their efforts, the employees will get tired of doing their best. They already know that whatever they present to the boss will not be ok. They will put less effort into their work. And so the cycle will only perpetuate itself.
This example is typical of the situation of many entrepreneurs or managers who during the coaching conversation, bring up the difficulties their employees have in living up to their expectations. Instead of reflecting on how they create their own reality, they are convinced that the problem is outside of them, generated by the employees.
Some very interesting experiments conducted in American schools and inspired by the studies of Robert Rosenthal, a Harvard Professor, clearly illustrate this phenomenon, known as the "Pygmalion effect". Two teams of teachers are assigned to two groups of students. The teachers do not know that the students have been randomly selected. The teachers of one group are told that students are gifted, they have extremely high IQs; the teachers of the other group are told that their students have learning difficulties. At the end of the year the students whose teachers had very high expectations reached above-average results for learning and development, while the results of the other group were lower than average.
The way in which we see the world and the beliefs we hold about people's ability - and therefore our expectations - influence our reality. Without having done experiments around it, I suspect that this also reflects our beliefs about our own abilities: depending on what we believe we are worth or can

do, we activate a series of behaviors that confirm our belief and create self-fulfilling prophecies.

REALITY YOU CAN TOUCH

Now we are really confused about what is real and that what is not. If we could at least have certainty with respect to the solidity of the world surrounding us ... But if we look at what matter is composed of, further doubts emerge about reality. Science has been investigating this issue for thousands of years, observing smaller and smaller pieces of matter. And the closer you look, under a microscope or through a particle accelerator, the more reality becomes something other than the observed object, almost unrecognizable, in fact.

The first to speak about the atom as a fundamental element of matter, was Democritus who said: "There is nothing but atoms and empty space, everything else is an opinion." The atom (Greek word meaning indivisible) was still an idea, there were no tools available to see it. Thousands of years later, equipped with the most modern tools, science has described the atom as mostly empty space in which there is a nucleus surrounded by electrons (Rutherford, Nobel laureate in Chemistry in 1908) and later as a nucleus with electrons revolving around it and following predetermined orbits (Neils Bohr, the father of quantum mechanics and Nobel prize winner for Physics in 1922).

We later discovered that this empty space is so vast that if the nucleus were the size of an orange, the boundaries of the atom would be about 30 km away from the fruit.

It means that bricks, tables, walls, books are made of 99% empty space. But we have the perception that they are "solid", they are compact. We are made of atoms too, as well as everything else. So

we are made mostly of empty space. It starts to get interesting, doesn't it? What, then, is real?
In both Buddhist and Hindu beliefs, the world we perceive with our senses is *maya*, an illusion. A limited, purely physical and mental reality, in which our awareness is trapped. Maya is seen as a veil that conceals the transcendent truth from which the illusion of physical reality originates. At present we don't have the means to be able to say that these assumptions are false, nor to corroborate the truth of the hypothesis that the world exists as an objective reality. The important thing is to challenge our certainties and be willing to consider other possible scenarios.

MIRROR, MIRROR ON THE WALL...

What are the personal implications? If there is not a single reality, but each of us gives a subjective interpretation of it, how can I tell who I really am? What is there about myself that I'm not aware of? Which limited reality of myself am I seeing just because I am imprisoned in a belief system and in the experiences of the past?
If I look in the mirror I can see the physical elements that are part of me and I can see the attitudes, perhaps even the emotions... it is an extremely vague picture and does not take into account what is probably evident to an outside observer but that I am unaware of. In addition, through the mirror I cannot access what is not immediately visible, such as my values or my needs, or the part that has not yet appeared in the conscious mind.
Knowing yourself is important to have a better understanding of the reality you create every day, because what you see today is interpreted through past experiences. Only if you are able to see the

color of the lenses you unconsciously wear every day, which color everything you perceive, will you be able to take them off and transform yourself and your world.
To help you with this activity, my advice is to ask others for feedback.

THE IMPORTANCE OF FEEDBACK

Feedback is a process in which, in a relationship, an observer offers to give his perception of an observed behavior and the (positive or negative) effect or consequence that such behavior has on the person he is observing. Receiving feedback is a precious moment of growth, a gift that allows you to have a greater understanding of your behavior and the impact it has on others, based on how it is perceived by other people, called "observers." Colleagues, employees, customers, relatives, friends, anyone can be an observer according to the aspects of yourself that you want to scrutinize. Receiving feedback is valuable because it opens a window on different perceptions others may have of you, allowing you to discover hitherto unknown aspects or to understand that some behaviors can be useful accelerators on the journey toward your goals, while others can hinder.
In the corporate world, especially in multinational companies, the feedback process is carried out regularly, so that each manager can receive feedback from their boss, colleagues and peers (sometimes customers are also included among the "observers").
Each observer is asked to complete a questionnaire and to give an assessment of the observed manager on a series of behaviors or skills, normally those that the company consider important to the manager's success and career advancement, such as strategic planning, conflict

management, influence and so on. The manager receives a confidential picture of how he is perceived in his professional role, which gives him interesting information on how to improve and make the most of his talents.

This kind of dedication to feedback occurs only in certain companies. Outside the working environment we are not accustomed to receiving useful feedback. And when we receive it, it's often in the form of criticism or otherwise it is very generic. Good feedback must be

- *timely*: it is better to know that our action has hurt someone as soon as the action happens and not after six months, for example.
- *relative to actions or behaviors and not to the person*: personal criticism creates defenses and does not generate growth, so it should be avoided. Pointing out which aspects of a behavior or which action have produced undesirable results makes feedback objective and makes it more effective.
- *specific*: the feedback must refer to a specific, observable behavior, and not to a personal interpretation of behavior. If I say to a friend "Last night, during our conversation, you suddenly stood up (observable fact) and went out, slamming the door (observable fact). I got the impression (so the effect your behavior had on me) you were angry and I felt sad" I offer my friend an opportunity to explain his intentions and his actions without embarrassing him or making him wrong. Maybe he got up and left because he remembered he had left the lights on and wanted to go home and turn it off. If I say, " Last night your irritated reaction (my interpretation of his feelings) showed me that

you don't care about listening to me (my guess)" I am judging my friend and trying to blame him. This normally closes the conversation or exacerbates the bad feeling.

- *sincere:* both positive and negative feedback must be honest. We must not exaggerate the positive comments so that they seem false, nor should we sugarcoat negative comments when we highlight a dysfunctional behavior.

EXERCISE: ASK FOR FEEDBACK

To get useful feedback, you must first select the observers. Whom would you like to receive feedback from?

- Father / Mother
- Husband/wife/partner
- Children
- Friends
- Colleagues
- Boss/former boss/mentor
- Collaborators/subordinates
- Customers/suppliers

Choose from six to twelve people who have had a prolonged experience with you (for example, a co-worker who has been working with you for only two months cannot give you relevant feedback, because his experience of you is limited).

Send them an email in which you ask them to answer a few questions to help you better understand some of your strengths and weaknesses, and in which you also ask them to be as honest and accurate as possible.

Select 6/8 questions from the following.

1. What do you think are my natural talents? How am I really special?

2. On what occasions did you see me demonstrating those talents (please tell me what I did and in what circumstances so that I can better understand)?
3. What do you think are the human qualities that best describe who I am?
4. What do you think is the approach I use to build relationships? How effective do you believe this approach is?
5. When did you see me successfully overcome obstacles? In your opinion, what resources did I tap into to do it?
6. What are the behaviors or attitudes that may hinder my effectiveness (at work, in relationships, in the pursuit of life goals... you can customize the question in the most useful way)?
7. What is the impact of these limiting behaviors or attitudes on me or on others?
8. In what ways do I sabotage myself, preventing myself from achieving my dreams and goals?
9. What should I start doing today that I usually don't do, to be more effective in... (work/ family/ leisure/ health management/ other)?
10. How do I communicate my emotions and express my feelings? How could I improve the way I do this with you?
11. How good do you think I am at saying no when it's needed and asking for what I need? What could I do to become better in this area?
12. How do I create trust in the people around me (or whom I work with)? What behaviors should I start (or should I stop) to create more trust?

Please feel free to design other questions that fit better with the feedback you would like to receive.

13. ______________________________

14. ______________________________

15. ______________________________

16. ______________________________

Once you have submitted your questions to your observers, giving them a deadline for their answers, you wait.

When you have received all the responses, put them together and read them with an open mind and without justifying yourself: remember that what your observers have shared is not reality, but their perception.

What is important for you is to notice what emerges from these comments and how you can turn feedback into an opportunity for personal growth. To do so, try asking yourself the coaching questions on the next page.

COACHING QUESTIONS:

What are the common themes when people describe your talents? (If there is uniformity in the responses it means that the perception that others have of you is homogeneous, a strong feature.)

____

____

____

What impressed you most in reading the feedback?

____

____

____

Find the connections between the feedback received and the key needs that you discovered in the Iceberg exercise. What are they?

____

____

____

Did you find there is a difference between the perceptions of the observers of when you are at work compared to those of your private life? What does this make you think?

____

____

____

3. How Do We Know What We Know

Reading the feedback received, which aspects would you need to change/improve to allow you to be more effective?

____

____

____

Use the diagram below to identify which behaviors you want to show more often, which you want to reduce or stop, and which new behaviors you want to start.

What behavior do you want to show more often?	**What behavior do you want to show less often?**
What behavior do you want to stop?	**What new behavior do you want to start?**

P.S. About Figure 3.2, you can see it in three ways: a section of a cube with a smaller cube inside; a large cube and a smaller cube on the outside; a large cube which lacks a corner with a small-cube shape.

4. The Software with Which We Are Programmed

"What can I do if I am who I am?" We started with this statement, which denies our responsibilities for our behaviors, for our reactions, sometimes for the choices we make. We believe that the DNA we have is responsible for the majority of our traits, as if it had the power to define "who we are".

Our body is a prodigious machine able to adjust our functions, to support us in case of need, to learn and improve our performance. Indeed, the way we function is largely outside our field of consciousness: many of the functions that our body performs are fully automatic, we don't need to think about them for them to be activated.

It is useful, however, to have a deeper understanding of how this machine operates so as not to become a slave to incorrect beliefs and automatic mechanisms. In this chapter, we will take a short journey to find out how the thoughts we entertain affect our lives and how some biological and neurological functions dominate our body.

(NEGATIVE) THOUGHTS "CONTROL" OUR BEHAVIORS

During the first six years of life, each of us acquires - at an unconscious level - the repertoire of behaviors necessary to become a functional member of society.

Children "download" from the environment and from their caretakers a wealth of information that, without a prior value judgment or verification, are installed directly in their subconscious mind. Paradigms and beliefs about what is right or not, what are the acceptable behaviors, what needs to be done to earn love and attention from others and, finally, important beliefs about themselves are downloaded. When a parent tells her child that he is smart and beautiful or stupid and undeserving, this information is stored as "fact" in the young subconscious mind.

Some physiological facts make this "download" extremely easy. The neocortex (the part of the brain where the capabilities of the language and thought reside) is perfected only when the child is around five or six. Before then the child has difficulty calibrating and evaluating the information.

In addition, the newborn baby produces almost all his brainwaves in the Delta frequency range and these waves remain present for the first few years of his life. Delta waves are the slowest in terms of frequency (ranging from 0.5 to 4 Hertz, while the faster Beta waves approach 34 Hertz) and are generally associated with empathy, the subconscious mind and a reduced sense of awareness. In adults this type of brain waves is often produced only during deep sleep. In their

early years children have an "open" mind in the sense that the information goes directly into the subconscious mind without being filtered.
The beliefs we download in childhood are then the "central command" of our behavior and most of them generate negative thoughts. Some behavioral psychologists have attempted to give a dimension to negative beliefs and have established that on average for each unit of positive beliefs there are about a hundred negative.
It follows that, while in our conscious minds we are convinced we are able to manage any situation, our powerful subconscious mind can simultaneously activate non-functional behaviors. This is why it is so difficult to make changes or see the effects of many behavioral training programs. Rationally we learn how to manage people better, how to speak in public effectively, how to delegate, but our subconscious mind hinders us by dropping negative thoughts that have been previously downloaded, such as "I am incapable", "I am ridiculous", "I am perfect" (a protective strategy of superiority).
Beliefs can be related to ourselves ("I am stupid "), to others ("my co-workers do not understand anything"), to concepts and circumstances ("money is dirty, earning a lot is evil"), to the outside world ("traveling is no longer safe"), to the future ("things will never work out"), to the past ("my parents never had time for me.")
While it is clear that these negative thoughts represent an inaccurate assessment of reality and create a series of emotions such as fear, anxiety, anger, jealousy and loneliness, it is less easy to recognize that they are born as an unconscious strategy to protect us from the possibility of rejection, humiliation or pain, the consequences of our basic needs when they go unmet.

Take for example the thought "I am stupid" and see what kind of protection it can give you:

- It reduces your expectations of yourself, so any mistake or failure will not be as traumatic as it may have been when you were a child.
- It also reduces the expectations others have of you (if you say it openly) because they will be led to believe that they can expect only mistakes and failures.
- It produces positive surprise in others, if you exceed their expectations (which were originally low as a result of your negative thinking).

We must remember that this whole process is subconscious. The mind is always working to protect you from pain and to create opportunities to solve your hidden emotional problems.
Here's a rundown of the main negative thoughts - about ourselves, about others, about the world, the future and the past - which we have to deal with.

a) Negative thoughts about yourself

They develop especially if, as a child, your concept of yourself was challenged. They manifest themselves in the form of a low self-opinion, so that no one will expect anything of you and you have a justification for avoiding risks, or in the form of excessive self-regard (a strategy of superiority), so that maintaining the acceptance by others becomes your most important occupation. Examples:

- I'm stupid
- I'm not worth anything
- I'm bad
- I am not … (good, handsome, tall, ...) enough
- I'm lazy
- I'm the black sheep

- I'm unreliable
- I always make mistakes
- I'm perfect (protective strategy of superiority)
- I'm always right (protective strategy of superiority)

b) Negative thoughts about others

They stem from the fear of making yourself vulnerable to the rejection of others. Also they shift the responsibility of changing to others, rescuing you from your share of responsibility. Examples:

- No one cares about me
- People are all selfish
- You're not here when I need you
- You never listen to me
- I can't trust anyone
- People think only about themselves

c) Negative thoughts about the world

When children receive enough love and protection, they develop a perception of the world as a safe and predictable place. If your safety needs have not been satisfied, you can perceive the world as an unsafe place and develop protection strategies that will dampen your ability to take any risk. Examples:

- (the city, America, the world…) is no longer safe
- In life there are only problems
- It's always the same, everywhere
- Life has no purpose
- We can no longer travel, it is dangerous
- Better not leave a safe place
- There are no opportunities out there.

d) Negative thoughts about the future

Their function is to protect you from failure, because with them you get ready for the fulfillment of the dire predictions you make.
Also they keep you on alert for circumstances or events that can threaten your self-esteem.
This type of negative messages will push you to a compensatory behavior of perfectionism, worry, agitation. Examples:

- "I know that I will never be able to ... (pass the exam, speak in public, etc.)"
- "Today all the bad things are happening to me"
- "I have so many things to do tomorrow!"
- "I will never make it in time with the presentation of the project"
- "I can't stop worrying"
- "The house will look like a disaster tonight"
- "I'll always be alone."

e) Negative thoughts about the past

They help you avoid taking ownership of the present, as they blame the past for your current low self-opinion. Examples:

- "I have never been treated well"
- "The school was a waste of time"
- "The professors were all incompetent"
- "My mother (father) never had time for me"
- "The school (my parents, my first girlfriend, etc..) has ruined my life. "

PATTERNS OF NEGATIVE THINKING

Negative thoughts can be classified as patterns which show how our mind "distorts" the perception of circumstances and events around us, and gives an interpretation of them that is not at all objective.
These patterns, identified by Aaron Beck and used in cognitive therapy, can be summarized as follows.

1. *Black-and-white thinking*: when you see only the extremes, without considering the grayscale that accompanies each interpretation. There is only good or bad, delicious or intolerable, intelligent or stupid. You notice it when you describe events with adverbs like "always" or "never": "My boss never gives me any acknowledgement", "You always have to belittle what I say."

2. *Ultra-generalization*: in this pattern you make an extreme generalization on the basis of an isolated event or a single piece of evidence. If a woman has a sudden emotional reaction, you conclude that "all women get agitated for nothing." If you are trying to mend your pants and you prick yourself with a needle then you conclude that "I will never be able to sew." Such generalizations can lead to a very restricted view of life. The language of generalization has keywords that you can recognize: "always", "every time", "nobody", "all", "any". The generalization ignores any opposite evidence, creating a stereotyped vision of the world.

3. *Mental filters*: you use a mental filter if you tend to see only one element of the situation (usually the negative) excluding all the many positive elements. You see a single detail and any condition is "read" through this filter. For example, your boss offers you praise for a job well done and asks if next time you can add a specific analysis. You take his request as criticism and ignore all the compliments you received.

4. *Jumping to conclusions*: you use this pattern when, instead of getting evidence and then drawing conclusions in a logical manner, you immediately jump to conclusions (usually negative) and then you trace back to find evidence that supports your

point of view. For example, a new person in an office who asserts that everyone is hiding something and claims to "know" that people are playing nice to manipulate him, is jumping to conclusions.

5. *Exaggerating*: when you exaggerate, you over-emphasize some small negative things of little importance, and in this way superficial mistakes become tragic failures: for example, a slight bone aching becomes osteoporosis. In contrast there is minimization, normally toward positive aspects. When considering your own skills or the benefits of some development, it's as if you look at them through the wrong end of a telescope which diminishes them.

6. *Foreseeing the catastrophe:* when you imagine and expect the worse scenario. When you see a small crack in the wall it means that soon the entire house will fall down.

7. *Mind reading*: this is when you make instant judgments about others, pretending to know how they feel and what their motivation is: "He does that only because he's envious", "She's afraid to show her feelings", "She gets nervous because she wants the promotion." When you dedicate yourself to mind reading you make your deductions on the basis of insights, impressions, fears or even past experience. These "clues" are not verified but you believe them all the same and you are led to act on the assumption that they are true. Mind reading is based on the process of *introjection*: you imagine that people feel your own emotions and react as you would. If you do not consider arriving late to be polite, you imagine that everyone else must think the same.

8. *Personalization*: you realize you're personalizing when you find yourself making comparisons with others that are unfavorable to you: "he plays football better than me", "I'm less attractive than Silvia", "I'm the slowest in the office." Sometimes the comparison is in your favor ("He's just stupid - and I'm smart"). In both cases, you question your value, then you continue to "check" it by comparing yourself with others. Another type of personalization is when you relate everything that happens around you to yourself. A mother blames herself when she sees her child getting sad, a man hears a colleague say that there is a risk the company will not reach the sales targets and he believe it's a criticism of his ability as a sales person.

9. *Labeling*: if you use this pattern on yourself or on others, you attach "labels" that are not supported by objective evidence: "She's whining," "He's a hypocrite", "I'm always gullible." Attaching labels in this way pigeonholes people (and ourselves) in roles that do not correspond to reality and prevents us from seeing people (and ourselves) as they really are.

10. *Statements with the word "must"*: in this pattern you think according to strict rules - created by yourself or others - that must be followed: "Children must go to bed early", "You should not talk about politics during a meal," "A good manager should arrive at the office before others and be the last to leave." The rules are always right and beyond question. In this way you judge and always look for wrong in others who exhibit intolerable behaviors, habits, or personality traits. A mother can have a rule that states that conscientious children "have to" phone home, when they are on vacation, at least three times a week. If the son goes on vacation and

forgets to call then it means that "He is an irresponsible son." This pattern is even more dangerous when it is addressed to ourselves: "I should be the perfect... (lover, wife, manager, father and so on)," "I should be able to find the solution to every problem," "I will not make mistakes," "I should never feel jealousy."

To become more aware of our negative thoughts and related patterns we don't have to do anything but listen to the voice in our heads.
Sometimes the voice labels us as incapable. Other times it says that no one loves us, or portends something terrible. And with these negative thoughts it triggers emotions in us – such as anxiety, anger, frustration, depression - which in reality are not only unproductive, but negatively "program" our way of seeing the world, preventing us from achieving our objectives by limiting our opportunities or by creating a separation between us and others.
If you need additional proof to grasp the profound effect our inner voice's negative (or positive) thoughts on have on our lives, just look at the diagram in *Figure 4.1*.

Figure 4-0-1 Different thoughts generate different emotions

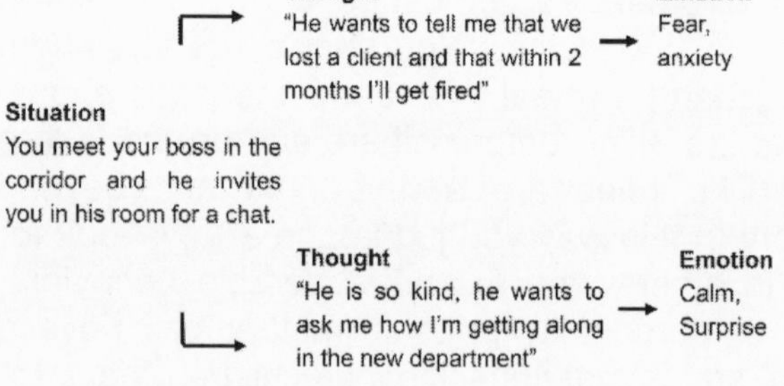

As Einstein said, we cannot solve our problems with the same thinking we used when we created them. We need to face them with a higher level of consciousness. If we want to dramatically reduce the activity of our incessant negative thinking we should, as we shall see in later chapters, take a quantum leap in our awareness and generate a personal transformation that will enable us to transcend the imprisonment of our unmet needs.
In the meantime, however, what you can do is analyze your negative thoughts, understand the link between them, your emotions and your behaviors, and ultimately learn to question them, to scratch away their patina of incontrovertible truth.
Here there are two exercises to achieve this.

EXERCISE: ANALYZE YOUR NEGATIVE THOUGHTS

For a few days, observe yourself in interactions with others or in dealing with whatever circumstance arises. Be careful to listen to your inner dialogue and notice if negative thoughts emerge. When this happens, notice without judgment what emotions are triggered by the negative thinking, and make notes. Finally observe what your behaviors are and note down these as well.
You can use the following table to jot down your negative thoughts, or you can draw it in your personal journal. Read the two examples in the table. Maybe they can be of help.

Circumstance	Negative thoughts	Emotions	Behaviors
I was invited to a party by a friend.	I do not know anyone; I will remain in a corner alone.	Embarrassment, shame, fear to be exposed.	I leave the party.
I asked my husband to water the garden while I was away and on my return I found that he hadn't done it.	I cannot count on him, as usual I always have to do things on my own.	Anger, frustration. I want to start up a quarrel.	I verbally attack my husband, and I do not talk to him for two days.
My colleague knew that there would be an important meeting, he didn't tell me and I was not present.	God knows what they said, I am always excluded, and my colleague does it on purpose to make me look	I feel dejected, disappointed and apprehensive. I feel victim of my colleague.	I do not explain how I feel; I ignore him and decide to sabotage my colleague on a project where my experience is essential.

4. The Software with Which We Are Programmed

Circumstance	Negative thoughts	Emotions	Behaviors

When you have finished analyzing the negative thoughts of a whole week, re-read what you wrote in the table and reflect.

- Is there anything that surprises you?
- Have you noticed recurring patterns of negative thinking?
- What do you notice with respect to the emotions that follow the negative thoughts?
- How useful are the behaviors that you enact because of the negative thoughts?

EXERCISE: QUESTIONING YOUR NEGATIVE THOUGHTS

A very useful strategy when we have negative thoughts is to question them and verify their accuracy. We may have had some of them for years, have come to accept them as truths and have avoided questioning them. Perhaps they were true once, in the past.

However, we feel they are still true today. The idea here is not to convince you not to believe a thought: we cannot consciously decide what to believe, and our beliefs are in fact the result of years of interactions between experience and perceptions.

What we can do is to provide our minds other information outside our paradigms and different from what we "know". The result could be to stop believing in something that we took for granted.

The following exercise is an adaptation of Katie Byron's transformational approach called "The Work". To begin this exercise, I ask you to identify a recurring negative thought that you can reflect on by asking twelve consecutive questions. Before you begin, read the following example.

Negative thought

I have to do everything alone, no one helps me.

Questioning the negative thought:

1. How do you behave toward yourself and toward others, when you believe this negative thought? *I make myself busy, I get angry with others who are not cooperative, but at the same time I am unwilling to accept help, I think it's useless. Those around me get frustrated and think I'm being unfair.*
2. What emotions stem from this thought? *I feel angry and disappointed by others, but it's as if I'd expected that, a sort of inevitability.*
3. If you had to identify where in your body this emotion was, where would it be? *Anger is in my sternum, while I feel the disappointment on my shoulders.*
4. What do you feel in this part of the body, due to the negative thought? *I feel warmth in the sternum, which makes breathing harder, and my shoulders are heavy, curving forward.*
5. What is the advantage for you of believing this negative thought? *This thought allows me not to rely too much on others and to automatically expect disappointment. I make myself the victim and I have a good reason if by any chance I cannot complete my task or my project: it is somebody else's fault because they haven't helped me.*
6. Can you find at least one example when this negative thought proved to be untrue? *I can find more than one. Once I had an idea that I could not achieve alone, and I found several people who helped me. Often when I ask for something of my life partner he goes out of his way to do what I ask.*
7. If you didn't believe this thought (imagine that this is possible), what would happen differently? *If I did not believe that nobody*

would help me, I would feel more relaxed asking for help explicitly. I would let people around me take care of me, I would have less of a "warrior" attitude and others would see my vulnerability.

8. If there was a good reason to stop believing in this thought, what would it be? *A good reason to stop believing this thought is that I would be less tired and I would have more free time.*
9. Try to write the negative thought upside down and make it positive. *In my life I am surrounded by people who are ready to give me a hand.* Now read it and reflect. Would this thought be as true as the other? Was there a time in your life when it was true? Or when someone might have thought it was true? *This thought is as true as the other. In fact, there have been times when I've received help, especially when I specifically asked for it.*
10. If you believed this new thought (imagine that this is possible), what would happen differently? *Probably I would notice all the little ways in which I receive help. A friend willing to listen to me and give me advice when I am in trouble, a pharmacist ready to bring the medicine to my home when I'm sick, my partner tidying the room.*
11. How would you behave toward yourself and toward others, if you believed this new thought? *I would be more optimistic and more appreciative toward others.*
12. What emotions would this new thought trigger? *Gratitude.*

At this point I think you will have understood the exercise and are ready to do it. Try to challenge your negative thought.

Negative thought

____

Questioning the negative thought:

1. How do you behave toward yourself and toward others, when you believe this negative thought?

____

____

2. What emotions stem from this thought?

____

____

3. If you had to identify where in your body this emotion was, where would it be?

____

____

4. What do you feel in this part of the body, due to the negative thought?

_________________-______________-________

____

5. What is the advantage for you in believing this negative thought?

____

____

6. Can you find at least one example when this negative thought proved to be untrue?

____

____

7. If you didn't believe this thought (imagine that this is possible), what would happen differently?

____

____

8. If there was a good reason to stop believing in this thought, what would it be?

____

____

9. Try to write the opposite of the negative thought and make it positive.

____

____

Now read it and reflect. Would this thought be as true as the other? Was there a time in your life when it was true? Or when someone might have thought it was true?

____

____

10. If you believed this new thought (imagine that this is possible), what would happen differently?

____

____

11. How would you behave toward yourself and toward others, if you believed this new thought?

____

____

12. What emotions would this new thought trigger?

____

____

How do you feel when you read the answers to this exercise? Have you discovered anything new with respect to your negative thoughts?

What the exercise aims to do is "infiltrate" new information that weakens the negative thoughts and makes a different thought reasonable and possible. Continue to do this exercise every time you hear yourself formulating negative thoughts. The repetition allows the brain to weaken certain neuronal connections and reinforce others.

THE MECHANISMS OF THE BRAIN

We have already alluded to the fact that the brain is a complex organ that receives a series of external stimuli which it tries to make sense of and is also responsible for our behavior.

Of all the information that the brain receives, as we have seen, only a fraction comes to our awareness, while the majority is discarded through the mechanism of inhibition, to prevent us from being distracted by unnecessary stimuli. From the remaining information, the brain forms vague images that are then processed and put together in association with other images that have been perceived in the past. Our past experiences, therefore, help to "create" our reality.

The brain processes stimuli and interacts with the rest of the body. The nervous system is a fantastic communication and control network. It has the functions of

1. perceiving the changes inside and outside the body,

2. interpreting and explaining the changes,
3. responding to interpretations by activating certain muscles and making sure that particular glands secrete hormones or other chemical elements into the blood stream.

To enable the nervous system to perform these three functions, it is made up of a vast circuit of cells that are interconnected.

The brain processes on average 40,000 neural stimuli per second. Each stimulus is dissected and the various key elements of the experience are separated. A neuron is matched to every single item, each "piece" of experience is then sent to the various areas of the brain that host neurons capable of processing elements of that specific nature.

If we look at an apple falling from a branch, the green color goes to one part of the brain, the shape to another, the movement to another and finally the neocortex associates the branch with the apple's fall. All information is analyzed and processed, and this fractionating and storage system allows the brain to process an infinite number of experiences.

When the input comes to be analyzed, the brain makes an attempt to couple it with elements stored in our memory.

If the pairing is successful, the elements of the input and the past event are "recognized". Otherwise, the search continues even if we have no knowledge that it's still at work. That's why some realizations, or insight, arrive at the most unexpected moments.

As the elements of the memory are encoded by the various parts of the brain involved (the parts connected to traumatic memories, for example, are stored in the amygdala) particular sets of neurons are activated (it is said that neurons "fire together").

Each element of this memory is represented by a group of neurons that are distributed in various brain regions but that "fire together" to reassemble that specific element. Once neurons representing the pieces of the same memory start to fire together (maybe even erroneously or prematurely), they will always fire together. If we repeat some activity in a coordinated manner, the relative combination of the neurons will strengthen its connection.

It is this process of "firing" that strengthens our behaviors until they become habits or patterns that, once learned, we repeat without needing to think.

If we go back in time to the moment when we learned to ride a bike, we may remember that the first time we struggled to stay balanced.

Perhaps we fell before we started pedaling and making it go straight. For some time, until the synaptic connections had strengthened, we rode uncertainly, being very careful to keep the handlebars straight, and we could only look straight in front of us or we'd lose concentration.

Later the action of pedaling and maintaining direction became so fluid that we began to travel with one hand, or to pedal while chatting or to carry someone on the back seat and manage to balance two people. When we succeed in an action without thinking about it, it means that the series of neurons associated with it are securely connected.

The limitation of this mechanism is that it also works for actions, reactions and emotions that we would not want to be tied together. If for example, the neurons connected to the action of pedaling were to fire together with those connected with "falling" and "pain", because maybe I'd had a few accidents, it is likely that I would begin to experience an emotion of fear every time I thought about the bike and may find it hard to learn to ride it.

THE AMIGDALA PREPARES US TO FACE THE DANGERS

To understand how the brain has evolved over the millennia, we can refer to the theory of the neuroscientist Paul McLean, according to which there are three distinct areas of the brain that have developed during the evolution of the human species: the reptilian brain, the limbic brain and the neocortex. At our birth, the reptilian brain (the reminder of our prehistoric past, the oldest part in terms of evolution, the part we share with reptiles) is being perfected.

The reptilian brain controls the vital functions such as heart rate, breathing, body temperature and balance, and it is also the organ that monitors our safety, always on the alert to identify potential hazards. This part of the brain tends to be somewhat rigid and compulsive.

The limbic brain (which developed after the appearance of mammals) can record memories of behaviors that produced pleasant or unpleasant experiences, so it is responsible for what we call emotions. In the structure of the limbic brain there are two glands, the thalamus and the amygdala, which we will meet later. The limbic brain is the base of our judgments of value, which, often unconsciously, exercise a strong influence on our behavior. In the human brain this area is perfected around the age of two or three.

The neocortex began to appear in primates and its importance peaked in the current human brain, with the typical form of the two hemispheres we normally see in representations of the brain. These hemispheres are responsible for the development of language, abstract thinking, imagination and consciousness. The neocortex is flexible and has endless learning skills.

These three parts of the brain do not operate independently, but have numerous interconnections through which they influence each other.
Other parts that play an important role in our brain are the thalamus and amygdala, two glands which, as we said, are present in the limbic brain: the thalamus helps to elaborate the information received from the sense organs and distribute it to other parts of the brain; the amygdala is a structure of interconnected neurons in the form of a double almond which has a key function in the processing and memorization of emotional reactions.
Normally when we receive an input (a stimulus from the outside), the information from the eyes, skin, ears or other sense organs is first directed toward the thalamus. The thalamus is like a huge gate through which only some information manages to enter, to be "passed" to the neocortex for further processing. Other information is blocked because it isn't useful or because it is in conflict with our paradigms.
At this point the item of information that passes through the gate is compared to those that have been recorded during our whole life, to see if it looks like something we have already seen or experienced. If the information is associated with some "neutral" or pleasant memory, then the impulse is sent to the neocortex. The neocortex processes the impulse, gives it meaning and sends the signal to the amygdala where a flow of peptides and hormones is released into the body to create emotions and action.
When, on the other hand, the input received is recognized as equal or similar to a danger that we have experienced in the past, then the thalamus sends the information directly to the amygdala, bypassing the neocortex - the "thinking" brain - and the amygdala reacts according to patterns stored in

the past, by flooding our body with chemicals and hormones, such as adrenaline, that prepare the body to react. The blood is channeled to the limbs, so that the body has the power to fight or to flee and our vision becomes entirely focused on the danger.

The first concern of the human brain is survival. It is therefore particularly determined to perceive, process, store and move to action in response to a danger from the surrounding environment. All areas of the brain and body are recruited and orchestrated to survive during a time of danger.

This global neurobiological participation in the response to danger is important if we are to understand how a traumatic experience can alter our normal functioning in such a pervasive way. Residual effects of a trauma – cognitive, emotional, social, behavioral and physiological – can have an impact on a person for years, even for life.

When we are born and until the age of two or three we still have not developed the language and the ability to calibrate and think about what happens to us. We are in our pre-verbal stage. As we have seen, we need love and protection from the surrounding environment, otherwise we will set in motion a strategy such as crying or shouting in order to satisfy our needs. When babies cry for food or affection, they are strengthening the neural pathways that help them to learn how to meet their needs physically and emotionally.

Children who do not receive answers to their cries and tears, and those whose cries are met with abuse (whether verbal, physical or emotional) learn different things. Short periods of moderate and predictable stress are not serious, indeed they prepare children to deal with the outside world. Our survival, in fact, depends on the ability to create a response to stress[9]. But prolonged periods of abuse, denial or constant combination of abuse and denial in the face of a particular need, create memories that are stored in an unconscious manner in the body and in neural circuits.

As the child grows, he will encounter other experiences and meet other inputs that will be classified as dangerous (for his life, his emotional balance or his social life), and these memories will combine with the pre-verbal ones until a large set of memories associated with fear is created. When those memories are triggered they will produce an unconscious and uncontrollable emotional reaction.

This automatic physiological mechanism of ours called "Amygdala hijack", described in *Figure 4.2*, has been functional to our survival for millions of years. Imagine the hominid in the jungle in front of a hungry tiger: he did not have time to think about which response was the most adequate to avoid the danger, he had to react immediately.

Even now, this automatic mechanism is valid in many cases: for example, it is what allows us to withdraw the finger we inadvertently put on a flame within a fraction of a second before it burns. Unfortunately it is also activated when it is not functional to our social situations, whether at home, at work or among friends and acquaintances.

The neuronal system have the special ability to create strong associations between a number of signals (for example, "roaring lion" and "danger") so that in the presence of these signals there is an immediate response.

---

[9] Jack Shonkoff, Deborah Phillips, Committe of Integrating the Science of Early Childhood Development, *From Neurons to Neighborhoods: the Science of Early Childhood Development*, National Academy Press, Washington, 2000

Figure 4-2 How the amygdala hijack works

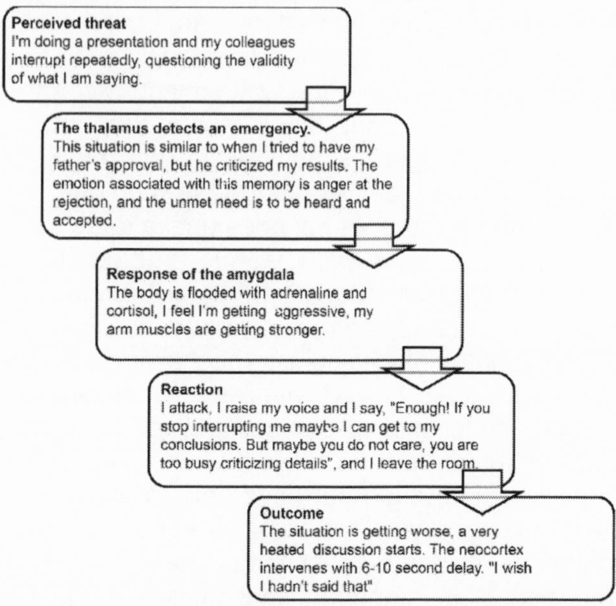

But the ability of the brain to develop and generalize, especially in front of a threatening stimulus, makes the human being vulnerable to developing false associations and false generalizations that can interpret an event as dangerous when it is not at all.

In the past I was very surprised at my automatic aggressive reaction whenever my partner made comments about my work or about a project that I was engaged in.

Although his comments were of course constructive, made with the intent to help me improve the work I was doing, and they were delivered in a neutral, non-negative way, as soon as I received them I could not restrain myself. I felt an acceleration of my heart rate, a contraction of my facial expressions and a change in my tone of voice, as if I could hardly hold back my anger. After

various occasions when this mechanism activated, I decided to notice and to analyze what was happening to me moment by moment.
I realized that when my partner spoke to me and offered me those comments, his facial expressions were similar to my mother's when she scolded me. My reaction, therefore, had nothing to do with his comments, but with the feeling of being "scolded", which was brought back to me by this visual reminder of my mother in circumstances where I had been mischievous or made some error.
It's like driving a car and looking in the rearview mirror. There is no creative power in these automatic reactions to people and events: we read what happens as if it was the memory of what happened to us in the past, and on the basis of this we continue to react in the way we always did, even if it is no longer functional.
Now we rarely encounter the kind of life or death danger that our sophisticated protection system was designed for.
Walking along the corridors of the company where we work, entering a store, wandering through the house, the people we interact with are hardly going to attack us. But we function constantly as if they might. The fact is that, over the years, many less "physical" but no less serious dangers for our well-being have been added to our repertoire of life threats. These are the threats to our emotional and social balance; the threats to our self-esteem, to our sense of worth, to our need to feel appreciated and loved, our need for inclusion, our need to be heard and so on, threats that are triggered by memories of times in the past when these needs were unmet.
When the amygdala hijack floods our body with chemical elements several things happen:

- Heart and breathing rate speed up. When your body is getting ready for action, it makes sure there is sufficient oxygen and blood in the main muscle groups and in the most important organs, so that you can fight or flee.
- Sweating increases. Sweating cools the body and it also makes the skin more slippery and thus more difficult to grab if a person or an animal tries to get you.
- You may feel nausea or stomach ache. When we face a danger, our body stops the processes and systems that are not necessary for survival. In this way it can direct the energy toward the functions that are critical for staying alive. Digestion is one of the processes that are not needed during a dangerous situation.
- You feel lightheaded or dizzy. Blood and oxygen go to the major muscle groups and this means that you will start to breathe faster to send oxygen where it is needed. This can cause hyperventilation, however, which can give you a feeling of vertigo. There is also a reduced supply of oxygen and blood in the brain.
- You may have a feeling of numbness or tingling in the limbs. In some parts of the body such feelings may be caused by hyperventilation. The tingling can be related to the fact that the hairs on our body stand up to increase our sensitivity to touch or movement. Tingling in the fingertips can be caused by the fact that the blood moves from the parts that are not needed during danger (such as fingers) to the muscle groups linked with survival (such as arms).
- You have enhanced vision. When you respond to the danger, your pupils dilate to let more light

in and to make sure you can see well. This reaction makes our environment seem brighter and sometimes less real.

- Your legs may feel heavy. As the legs prepare to take action (fight or flight), the muscle tension grows, while the level of blood in these muscles is also increasing, causing the sensation of heaviness.

In these ways the body is physiologically able to respond immediately to imminent danger.

EXERCISE: IDENTIFY WHAT HIJACKS YOUR AMYGDALA

For one week, try to identify and analyze all situations in which you respond to certain stimuli with an automatic emotional reaction that you cannot control and which usually manifests itself in aggressive behavior (for example: you raise your voice, shout, bang your fist on the table, attack either verbally or physically, get angry, throw the phone etc…) or passive behavior (for example: you become quiet, you avoid saying what you want, you isolate yourself, you leave, you cry).
Fill in the table on the following page as if it were a diary of your emotional reactions.
Reflect on this exercise.
When you read your notes, does anything strike you?

____

____

Compare the results of this exercise to the one related to the iceberg model on your key needs. Can you find links between events, or between the needs that you felt were endangered? What do these links reveal to you?

Triggering event or circumstance	**Reaction: with what behavior did I respond to this event or circumstance?**	**What emotions did I feel?**	**What need, if I think about it now, did I feel was endangered?**	**Which past event do I I unconsciously associate the triggering event**
Example: my boss said that I will not get the promotion I expected.	I told him surely no one is smarter than me, but others get promoted while I do not, this is not fair.	Anger, frustration, lack of recognition.	Proving that I am good, I'm worth it.	Although I studied a lot, there was a teacher who was never happy with my results.

4. The Software with Which We Are Programmed

Can you identify situations in the past to which you can link the majority of your automatic emotional reactions (as if these situation were nodal points from which different types of automatic reactions derive)? What are they?

____

____

DO I RESPOND OR DO I REACT?

Two million years ago, when the ability to activate an automatic response for survival was developed, the "fight" reactions manifested as aggressive behavior, those of " flight" as physically moving away from danger, and those of "freeze" as an actual immobilization of the body with the aim of concealing oneself.

Ethology has shown that when the prey remains motionless during a threat it is more likely to remain undiscovered, because the visual cortex and the retina of carnivore mammals primarily detect moving objects rather than colors; immobility can also increase the chances of survival by inducing the predator to weaken the grip on its "frozen" prey, supposing it to be dead and allowing it an opportunity to run away.

These kind of reaction is exhibited by humans when they feel they don't have a chance either to escape or to win a fight.

In our time these atavistic responses persist, but the fight, flight and freeze modalities include a much wider range of behaviors. For example, a fight reaction can show up as argumentative behavior or sarcasm and the flight reaction can be expressed by closing in on oneself. But we repeatedly experience automatic responses, generated by fear, that are not appropriate.

In some cases we live for long periods in a condition of hyperactivity of the amygdala, and our body remains in a state of continuous excitement and stress, with serious consequences for body and mind. Some simple kinds of stress can be managed easily and quickly to restore our body to homeostasis (the condition of internal stability).
With the more complex stress of modern society, however, where several factors and people are involved, the danger seems unavoidable and its relative state continues indefinitely, jeopardizing the system instead of helping it.
Each of us developed automatic coping strategies in childhood that worked and produced results. And for different events, a person may have different strategies. If I think of my childhood, for example, when a child more or less my age stole my toys or tried to dominate me, my reaction was to fight. When at home, on the other hand, I listened to the arguments of my mother and my father and I heard them shouting, I would run and hide in my room (flight).
Figure 4.3 lists some types of fighting, fleeing and freezing behavior, some of which you are probably familiar with.
It may be helpful for you to reflect on what strategies you have adopted in different threatening or dangerous situations, in the course of your life, and how the reactions you have today resemble those that you developed as a child. This awareness, in the moment in which the uncontrolled reaction emerges, can help you identify it and understand that you're only repeating a defensive pattern that you learned as a reaction to a state of danger.

Figure 4-3 Expressions of a defensive behavior

Fight	Flight	Freeze
Argumentative behavior. Sarcasm, ridicule. Hostile criticism. Lack of listening. Hostile silence. Open or passive attack. Violent acts (for example smashing the telephone or punching the wall). oversights, delays, "distractions" (passive-aggressive behaviors).	Moving away physically from the aggressor (exiting the room, smashing the phone). Leaving the situation emotionally (closing in on oneself, abstracting oneself, being lost in one's own thoughts). Crying. In extreme cases, alcoholism or abuse of drugs.	Inability to react. Dissociation. State of shock.

COACHING QUESTIONS

Which frequent negative thoughts "control" your life and the choices you make?

____

____

____

What are the consequences?

____

____

____

Go back to the Coaching Questions in Chapter 3 and to the unmet needs you found… is there a link between the unmet needs and the negative thoughts?

____

____

____

Which negative thinking patterns are responsible for the sabotaging system that you use to protect yourself?

____

____

____

What did you learn about your emotional reactions of fight, flight and freeze?

____

____

____

5. The Intelligence of the Heart and Our Emotions

SMART HEART

I remember as a child I "knew" which people were good and which were potentially dangerous for me. By the term dangerous I mean people who don't necessarily have good intentions or who could cause me problems. I had a natural instinct for recognizing what would do me good and what wouldn't. It still works for me today, and it's also useful for protecting the people I love. I particularly remember a man to whom one of my best friends introduced me one day as her future business partner. It took only a five-minute conversation for me to warn my friend: be careful, I don't like this person, I suspect that he will cause you trouble. There were no rational elements on which I could base my response.

Nothing of what he told me was objectionable or could arouse a suspicion of bad intentions. How could I explain to her that she had to trust my intuition? Of course my friend underestimated the alert. She reassured me that this person was a family acquaintance, who had many contacts abroad to develop her business. He represented a great opportunity for her. I could not do anything other than advise her to be careful. Only a few years later we would witness the endless problems this man's behavior caused both the company and my friend, who was the firm's legal representative and had to go through a terrible time with lawyers and accountants.

Has it ever happened that you "know" something without any rational evidence? Has it ever happened that, in the moment of making a choice, you have felt your heart and mind going in two different directions? Maybe when you analyze the situation, and think about the pros and cons in order to make a rational choice, you realize that the right choice is to follow the heart? And how many proverbs and aphorisms are there that give credit to the heart for its many skills? "The way is not in the sky. The way is in the heart", "The heart has reasons that reason does not understand", "As a man thinks in his heart, so is he", "There is no instinct like that of the heart"... The heart is also used as a symbol of our intuition and moral judgment. We use phrases like "the heart told me" or "listen to your heart before you make a decision" and generally those who say such things are not inviting you to physically perceive your heartbeat, but to use the heart as a metaphor for intuition. Also we associate the heart with our emotions: "lionheart" indicates courage; "my heart hurts" means I am sad.

Do these concepts of the heart as a place of emotions and an intuitive knowledge have some substance? Is there truth in those sayings and

ancient wisdom? Many populations in the distant past believed that the home to thoughts, emotions or the soul was the heart. Only in relatively recent times has the brain been identified as the center of these activities. In your opinion who is right?
Scientific studies now show that such awareness originates from a team effort between mind and body, and the heart plays an important role in this process. We are used to thinking of the heart as a muscle that pumps blood and keeps our circulation going until we die. Over a period of seventy years, it beats 100,000 times a day, 40 million times a year. But think for a moment: what makes your heart beat for the first time, in the fetus when the brain is not yet formed?
What makes the heart beat the first time? Scientists still do not know the answer to this question and use the word autorhythmic to indicate that the heartbeat is self-initiated from the heart itself. In a child not-yet born there is a heart before there is a brain and even when the brain begins to develop, the reptilian brain, which deals with all the automatic functions, appears first and then comes the limbic brain, which oversees the emotional centers with the amygdala and the thalamus. Only later, from the age of three onwards, does the neocortex begin to reach completion, with the logical thinking skills related to it. So the child develops the heart, then the emotional brain and only later the rational brain.
Recently some neuroscientists[10] made an interesting discovery. They found that the heart has

---

10 Andrew Armour, Jeffrey Ardell, *Neurocardiology*, Oxford Univertisty Press, Oxford, 1994; Paul Pearsall, *The Heart's Code*, Broadway Books, 1998, Rollin McCaty, Mike Atkinson, Dana Tomasino and Raymond Trevor Bradley, "*The Coherent Heart. Heart-Brain Interactions, Psychophysiological Coherence and the Emergence of System-Wide Order*",

its own independent nervous system (the "heart brain") consisting of approximately 40,000 neurons. This nervous system of the heart continuously sends information to the brain, creating a two-way communication that exchanges information with the central nervous system. The information exchanged in this way has an impact on various functions in the amygdala, the thalamus, and the neocortex. In particular, the nervous system of the heart allows it to learn, remember, and make decisions independent of the brain.

Before the '70s and the studies of John and Beatrix Lacey of the Fels Research Institute in Ohio[11], it was believed that the nervous system linked our heart to the brain, and that the brain was in "control". John and Beatrice Lacey showed that when the brain sends orders to the heart, the heart does not automatically obey, but rather responds following its own distinct logic. In addition, the heart seems to send messages to the brain that the brain not only considers, but obeys, and it seems that these messages from the heart influence the behavior of a person.

The communication between the heart and brain occurs in the following ways:

- neurologically (through the transmission of nervous impulses)
- biochemically (through hormones and neurotransmitters)
- biophysically (through electromagnetic waves)
- energetically (through interactions of magnetic fields)

Integral Review, Vol. 5, December 2009, www.heartmathbenelux.com/doc/McCrat yeal_article_in_integral_review_2009.pdf.

[11] John and Beatrix Lacey, in Percy Black, *Physiological Correlates of Emotions*, Academic Press, New York, 1970.

The HeartMath Institute in Boulder Creek, California, is an organization connected with Stanford University that has been studying the heart and its impact on health for about twenty years. The studies and experiments published by the Institute, which can be found at www.heartmath.org, offer us a very complex and intriguing picture of the heart.
The Institute's studies show that the human heart generates an electromagnetic field, wider than those created by any other organ of the body, and whose magnetic component is approximately 5,000 times more powerful than the one generated by the brain. It not only permeates every cell, but it radiates outside of us and is perceived by those who are in its communication range. The electromagnetic field of the heart can be measured with magnetometers, while the patterns of electrical information generated by the heart can be reported by the electroencephalogram (EEG). The heart, in its beating, emits electromagnetic pulses that we can imagine as a series of waves whose rhythms influence other parts of the body, such as the rhythm of the brain waves, the blood pressure, and the respiration. It is as if the heart functions as a metronome in a continuous process of synchronization[12].
The Heartmath Institute has also shown how different emotions alter the rhythmic cadence of the heartbeat, helping to generate a more or less coherent pattern of the heart rhythm and, thanks to the effect of the synchronization of the heart, of that of the rest of the body.

---

[12] Rollin McCraty, *The Energetic Heart: Bioelectromagnetic Communication Within and Between People*, in P.J. Rosch and M.S. Markov, *Clinical Applications of Bioelectromagnetic Medicine*, Marcel Dekker, New York, 2004.

Emotions such as anger or frustration are associated with a messy and incoherent pattern of the heart rhythm. In contrast, emotions such as love and appreciation are associated with a coherent and orderly pattern. Changes in heart rhythm are reflected in changes of the electromagnetic field of the heart.

The measurements of this electromagnetic field, together with the monitoring of the subjects of the study, have shown that there is a link between the emotions of love, appreciation and joy and a particular type of psycho-physiological functioning, which gives rise to:

- greater efficiency and harmony in the activity of the body
- reduction of mental dialogue and perception of stress, improvement in performance and emotional equilibrium, improved clarity, and greater ability to access one's own intuition.

THE IMPACT OF EMOTIONS ON MAN

The key emotions such as happiness, appreciation, compassion, love and care improve hormonal balance and the response of the immune system. It has been demonstrated that they reduce the activity of the sympathetic nervous system (the part of the nervous system that accelerates the heart rate, constricts blood vessels and stimulates the release of stress hormones in readiness for action) and increase the activity of the parasympathetic nervous system (the part that slows the heart rate and relaxes the internal systems of the body), thus improving the overall effectiveness of the system.

The opposite is true when dealing with emotions such as anger, frustration or stress. They create a messy rhythm, which in turn gives rise to chain reactions in the body: venous constriction,

increased blood pressure, energy dispersion. If we stay in these emotional states for too long, or if they occur repeatedly, the result can be increased blood pressure (which increases the risk of heart problems and strokes).
The emotions of frustration, agitation, hostility, resentment, anxiety, worry, and all those that descend from primary emotions of anger and fear (*Figure 5.1*), represent the response of body and mind to events or circumstances that push us out from a condition of equilibrium.

Figure 5-1 Primary, Secondary and Tertiary Emotions

Primary emotions	Secondary emotions	Tertiary emotions
Love	*Affection*	Adoration • Fondness • Liking • Attractiveness • Caring • Tenderness • Compassion • Sentimentality
	Lust	Desire • Passion • Infatuation
	Longing	Longing
Joy	*Cheerfulness*	Amusement • Bliss • Gaiety • Glee • Jolliness • Joviality • Joy • Delight • Enjoyment • Gladness • Happiness • Jubilation • Elation • Satisfaction • Ecstasy • Euphoria
	Zest	Enthusiasm • Zeal • Excitement • Thrill • Exhilaration
	Contentment	Pleasure
	Pride	Triumph
	Optimism	Eagerness • Hope
	Enthrallment	Enthrallment • Rapture
	Relief	Relief
Surprise	*Surprise*	Amazement • Astonishment • Shock • Stunned
Anger	*Irritability*	Aggravation • Agitation • Annoyance Grouchy • Grumpy • Crosspatch Offended
	Exasperation	Frustration
	Rage	Anger • Outrage • Fury • Wrath • Hostility • Ferocity • Bitter • Hatred • Scorn • Spite • Vengefulness • Dislike • Resentment
	Disgust	Revulsion • Contempt • Loathing • Superior

	Envy	Jealousy • Envious
	Torment	Torment
Sadness	*Suffering*	Agony • Anguish • Hurt
	Sadness	Depression • Despair • Gloom • Glumness • Unhappy • Grief • Sorrow • Woe • Misery • Melancholy
	Disappointment	Dismay • Displeasure
	Shame	Guilt • Regret • Remorse • Humiliated • Mortified
	Neglect	Alienation • Defeatism • Dejection • Embarrassment • Homesickness • Humiliation • Insecurity • Insult • Isolation • Loneliness • Rejection
	Sympathy	Pity • Sympathy
Fear	*Horror*	Alarm • Shock • Fear • Fright • Horror • Terror • Panic • Hysteria • Mortification
	Nervousness	Anxiety • Suspense • Uneasiness • Apprehension (fear) • Worry • Distress • Dread

Source: W. Gerrod Parrott, Emotions in Social Psychology, Psychology Press, Philadelphia, 2000

This happens when the perception of what is happening - which is totally subjective - it is not in line with our expectations and we are not able to manage our reaction to disappointment.

It is through these emotions that we are able to react (if the event or circumstance is a danger) to get what we want. They are the engine of many of our actions.

When we feel them, our body is filled with adrenaline and other chemicals - such as norepinephrine and cortisol - that increase the heart rate, increase muscle tension and accelerate our breathing (*Chapter 4*). However, once activated, these substances can remain in the system for hours, even after the disruptive event has ended.

A prolonged state of this type of emotion, and the relative high level of cortisol that follows, resets the thermostat inside the brain and suggests to the body that maintaining a high production of this hormone is normal. The consequences of long periods governed by these emotions can be: reduction of immune activity, reduction of the use of glucose, promotion of osteoporosis, reduction of muscle mass, inhibition of the skin's growth and regeneration, fat accumulation, problems with memory and learning, destruction of brain cells.

When I worked in the Internet industry, I remember that we had a frenetic pace of work and long hours (even 14 hours a day for several weeks), constant pressure for the expected results and open or covert competition between colleagues. Despite the passion for the work and the satisfaction it gave me, I often felt emotions of irritation, agitation, anger, anxiety, disappointment, insecurity, alarm and apprehension. Not only that. When I went out in the evening with friends or colleagues, or if I talked to my mother or those who I loved, our conversations converged on my work and I often complained about the stressful condition in which I found myself. Alas, thoughts trigger emotions even in the absence of a specific event, so I found myself immersed in the same state of mind throughout the day (and often my mind continued to process what had happened during the night).

In addition to developing a very irritable mood, my blood pressure at some point reached levels so high that I fainted in the street. My hypertension started at that time, when I was only 36.

Now that I live a life far more full of "healthy" emotions, and that the new profession I have chosen gives me infinite joy, when I visit companies to which I provide coaching and organizational development services, I see the person I used to be widely replicated in a good number of managers. Conditions of continued stress (whether people are aware of it or not) can only adversely affect their health, as well as producing the opposite of what every company would like to obtain from its employees: a decrease in performance and in the skills of focusing, vision and collaboration.

BIOLOGY OF EMOTIONS

The scientist who, more than any other, has devoted his energies to understanding emotions and consciousness, so as to become one of the most important neuroscientists in this field, is Antonio Damasio. A graduate in medicine, born in Portugal and now a U.S. resident, Damasio has founded some research laboratories at the Iowa University that are considered now a point of reference for the study of nervous phenomena underlying cognitive processes.

Damasio proposes a distinction between emotions and the inner experience of emotions (feelings). An emotion is the set of the changes occurring in the brain and body triggered by a stimulus that may be unconscious. The emotion, thanks to these changes, can be "seen" by others. The word "feeling" is used to describe a private and inner experience of an emotion.

Imagine you have an appointment with a potential new customer and you want to make a good impression. After you have met him in the reception area of his company building, you climb the stairs to his office. Suddenly your foot slips on the stairs: you sway and risk falling backwards. It lasts just a moment and you manage to keep your balance. But the danger of falling has caused some emotions: first, the fear that has stimulated the amygdala to help your body to handle the situation; and immediately afterwards, a sense of shame because the new client might have considered you clumsy and you want to be seen as a professional completely in control of yourself and your environment.

Although no one can observe the feelings of another person, some aspects of the emotions that generate the feelings can be seen (such as a change in the facial muscles).

The customer, therefore, might have noticed your face twitching and your eyes and mouth opening wide. Perhaps he observed that you are mildly flushed or that you bowed your head soon after. He can make assumptions but has no idea what is going on inside you in terms of feelings.

In addition, the mechanisms underlying the emotions can be completely beyond our awareness. The whole procedure that leads up to the emotional event can start without you being aware of the initial cause or the intermediate stages. Very often we do not have any idea why we feel happy or unhappy, frightened or angry. The unconscious processes by which emotions are unleashed may explain why they are so hard to mimic in a credible way.

We cannot control our emotions with our will. We can try to prevent the expression of an emotion (and we can manage it, at least in part), but the most we can achieve is the concealment of an external manifestation, without being able in any way to block the automatic changes occurring in the bowels and elsewhere in the body. The only exceptions are represented by the control of breathing, which can affect blood pressure and heart rate, or by techniques such as biofeedback[13].

---

[13] Biofeedback, through specialized equipment, measures the physiological changes – for example the electroencephalographic rhythms, muscle tension, skin temperature, heart frequency – in a way that allows the subject to adopt control strategies to manage the monitored functions voluntarily.

We can partially suppress facial expressions, but we cannot eliminate our emotions. Our inner feelings are proof of this.

When, during the workshops that my company offers to individuals and companies, the facilitator asks participants what emotion they are feeling, they often respond that they have no emotions at all.

This is probably an illusion caused by our lack of familiarity with the emotions and the limited vocabulary we use to describe them. Most of us live mainly in our "head" and were never trained to listen to our own body, and are not able to feel what changes are taking place and are happening continuously.

We can describe the emotions as complicated sets of chemical and neural responses that form patterns. Their function is to control, that is, to create more advantageous circumstances to the organism. In a nutshell, they help our body to maintain life[14]. They are biologically determined processes, that have been perfected during the evolutionary history, and that depend on the innate mechanisms of the brain, mechanisms that can be operated automatically, without deliberate consciousness.

The biological function of emotions is very important. First of all they produce a specific reaction to a situation, such as avoiding a hazard, pushing oneself into action, becoming open or cautious. In addition, they regulate the internal state of the organism so that it is prepared for the specific reaction (as we have seen in the functioning of the brain and the amygdala).

To use Damasio's words:

---

[14] Antonio Damasio, *The Feeling Of What Happens*, Vintage-Random House, 2000.

> *At their base, emotions are part of the homeostatic regulation and prepare us to avoid the loss of integrity which is a precursor of death or death itself, as well as to support a source of energy, shelter, or sex. And as a result of powerful learning mechanisms, such as conditioning, the emotions of all the nuances in the end help to connect the homeostatic regulation and the "values" of survival in numerous events and objects in our autobiographical experience. Emotions are inseparable from the idea of reward or punishment, pleasure and pain, backward and forward movement, personal advantage and disadvantage. Inevitably emotions are inseparable from the idea of good and bad*[15]*.*

In summary, emotions arise when we experience an object or an event - be it external or internal to ourselves - or when we "think" about an object or an event. The biological bases of emotions are predetermined, but the ways of inducing emotions may vary, depending on the experience of the environment we have built up and by the learning this has caused.
So the emotions remain "stuck" to the perception of specific details, objects and situations, directly observed or living only in our mind.
In the Western culture there is little familiarity with emotions. Nevertheless they play an important role in our lives and in our social interactions. I suggest therefore an activity to become familiar with your emotions and discover something more about yourself. This exercise will also be useful later in

[15] *Ibidem*, p. 55.

the book, when you will try to make some personal transformations.

EXERCISE: RECOGNIZE YOUR OWN EMOTIONS[16]

Part one: the emotion I feel

Below you will find some statements to be completed. They will help you to develop the vocabulary of emotions and become emotionally more aware. For each one, make a list of emotions. Write your answers quickly, without thinking too much and using one word for every emotion. You can do this exercise with a partner.

At work

When I get ready to go to work I often feel

____

At the end of the day I often feel

____

While I'm at work I often feel

____

With my boss I feel

____

When my co-workers disappoint my expectations I feel

____

When my co-workers don't do what I ask I feel

____

When employees or customers don't listen to me I feel

____

When I think about the possibility of finding a (another) job I feel

____

[16] Developed from Nathanien Banden's idea of "sentence completion"

5. The Intelligence of the Heart and Our Emotions

Thinking that I can have an impact on my staff, either positive or negative, makes me feel

____

Family Life

With my/ spouse / partner I feel

____

With my children I feel

____

With my parents I feel

____

With my family I feel

____

When I think of the mistakes I have made I feel

____

When I think of what I have learned in my life I feel

____

When I think about my recent past I feel

____

When I think of the next few days I feel

____

When I think of the next few months I feel

____

When I think of the next few years I feel

____

Second part: how I felt

In elementary school I felt

____

In middle school I felt

____

In high school, I felt

____

In college I felt

____

With my childhood friends I felt

____

When .... died I felt

____

The first time I met .... I felt

____

When I made a serious mistake I felt

____

Now look back at *Figure 5.1* and see if some of the emotions that you wrote down could be better described with other words.
To complete this exploration try replacing your words with those in the figure.

THE EMOTIONAL HISTORY WE COME FROM

Emotions are the driving force of our behavior. They train our body to act and respond to the external environment. We should know them very well and be at ease with them, they are our companions and our allies: they try to move us toward situations of safety and enjoyment. At times, however, it doesn't seem so; it seems instead that they work against us. Think of a person who is about to make an important presentation and begins to blush. His emotion is clear to the audience. What advantage does he get when blushing? Everyone can see this immediate reaction on his face and realize that he is nervous, and this certainly does not help the success of the presentation or the presenter's ability to demonstrate confidence and to persuade.
What you need to understand is that the emotions are part of a complex protection system, which derives from the program that we downloaded in our childhood and have updated during life. It is based on the stories we began to believe before we had a choice; stories we heard from our parents and people around us; stories about how we should be, but are not; stories that we constructed to make

sense of what was happening around us and that we have come to accept as reality; stories that the voice told us and maybe is still telling us to this day. So, to simplify, let's imagine that the presenter in the example developed an unmet need of unconditional love in childhood because his father continuously sent him messages that he interpreted as "you're not good enough to deserve my love." Imagine that, in order to win his father's love, the baby presenter adopted the strategy of accomplishing amazing endeavors to continually prove his talent. A fear of failure is built in to this strategy, because failure would symbolically mean losing love. This mechanism, which is so old that the adult presenter doesn't even remember its origins, is encoded in his program of survival through the satisfaction of a need that was frustrated in the past and after thirty years still resurfaces. And the man's emotions are there to remind him that there is a fear, a fear of failure that underlies his performance, at least until he is able to see it for what it is, to understand it and accept it. This is a possible story – that failure for the presenter will result in a loss of love that threatens his very survival. Each of us has created several such stories in the course of our life. The important point is that these stories are fantasies, not reality. And, more importantly, they do not reflect who we truly are.

If we put ourselves in the position of the observer we can capture the manifestation of our emotions and make them more familiar. We can also understand the roots of our emotions more frequently and better understand how the first years of our lives shaped them. Try to go back in time. What was the emotional climate of your family? Did your parents express their emotions or did they repress them? Did they openly speak about fear, joy, anger, pain? Did they help you to understand your emotions when they arose? Did they hug you when you cried or did they get angry? Were you taught that such emotions should not be expressed?

In my family my father always seemed a sphinx. It was very difficult for me to read his emotions. I had friends who regularly visited my home, some even joined us on holidays, and I remember one of them came up to me and said, "After twelve years, I just saw your dad laughing for the first time." He was a shy man and, especially in public, he was very restrained.

My mother has always been like a rollercoaster, with ups and downs, and many excesses. She was euphoric or depressed, furious or suffocating. With people outside the family, she was predominantly euphoric if she found an environment where she felt she was the center of the attention, or angry if someone had ideas different from hers. As she got older she lost a bit of her energy, but these are still the basic aspects of her behavior.

As a child, what I learned from my parents was that expressing joy and fun makes you attractive to others, it makes you look nice and everyone wants to be around you. I also learned that if you want to get something, exploding with anger and being aggressive helps. I also learned that sadness should not be shown, because it makes you feel weak.

What did you learn from your parents about emotions?

Each child builds strategies to avoid those feelings they find it hard to deal with. For example, I tried as hard as I could to keep a low profile and to obey to my mother. The idea of seeing her infuriated was devastating for me.

I also adopted the strategy of transforming sadness into anger. Sadness, in fact, made me weak (in my eyes) while anger gave me a sense of possibility and control, a sense of action instead of submissiveness. I believe that neither friends nor relatives had ever seen me cry, until a few years ago, when I started my journey of personal transformation. I understood my emotions and my feelings and I began to undo the program, based on needs and fears, that I had installed many years ago.

I invite you to think about the way you responded to and managed the feelings you were uncomfortable with.

Your parents are not to blame for how you grew up and the program you learned. Unfortunately, they had been programmed in their infancy too and they did their best with the level of consciousness they had. There is no doubt that they loved you, that you were an extraordinary event in their lives, and that all they wanted was to protect you. But they could only accomplish this within the limits of what they were taught and had the opportunity to learn.

What is certain is that people of my generation and younger (people in their thirties and forties), compared to older generations, have a higher level of self-awareness. And in subsequent generations this self-awareness will continue to expand.

TO SUPPRESS OR TO BURST?

What most of us have learned, with few exceptions, is that there are emotions that need to be suppressed, deleted, concealed. For some people, especially men, these include sadness. Until adolescence, as demonstrated by William Frey[17],

---

[17] William H. Frey, *Crying: The Mystery of Tears*,

biochemist at St. Paul-Ramsey Medical Center in Minnesota, baby boys and baby girls cry the same amount of tears. When they grow older males drastically reduce their crying compared to females. In our culture, in fact, a man's crying is perceived as a sign of weakness. How many times have you heard "Boys don't cry"? Children hear this so many times that obviously, when they get to puberty, the cultural conditioning has a deep influence on them. There is a primitive root in this warning. Our ancestors knew that tears are associated with physical pain and in their experience, therefore, the man who cried was physically weaker than the one who, with the same wounds, could hold back the tears. The strong man was treated with respect, had charisma and was more likely to become the "boss". In addition, well yes, he was more likely to mate and reproduce, and we know that our main purpose as human beings living on the first level of consciousness (that of survival) is to reproduce and transfer genetic material to the next generation.

Today, fortunately, our reproductive capacity does not depend on the man's physical strength anymore. Our cultural and psychological evolution requires greater ability to understand and use emotions, including the ability to develop empathy with others.

An emotion that is, instead, often suppressed by women is anger, and this mechanism too starts from an ancient legacy because it has always been considered socially inappropriate for women to express anger.

In spite of everything, the (false) stories we tell ourselves even today make us act as our ancestors would have done. Isn't it time to update our system?

Winston Press, Minneapolis, 1985

Emotions are too often managed by us human beings in an unproductive way, either by suppressing them (as my father did) or by bursting (like my mother). Imagine these two modes as a continuum:

Suppression (implosion) ⟷ *Explosion*

Suppression damages our health and our psychophysical balance. In fact, even if we eliminate the "external manifestation" of the emotion, the emotion is there and gets trapped in our body. Often suppressing it at a given time makes it come out later, when it is completely out of context, as might be the case of an employee who cannot express anger at his boss, but when he gets home becomes aggressive toward his wife, for no reason.

We try to suppress a feeling when we are not able to live with the discomfort that it causes us or when we are scared of it.

To avoid coming into contact with this feeling we put various strategies to use:

- we ignore it
- we get excessively busy with something
- we overindulge in food, drugs, work, sex, or something else
- we eat food with lots of sugar or fat
- we do sports compulsively
- we continuously analyze and intellectualize
- we bury the emotion behind a mask of apparent serenity

In the long run the suppression of emotions damages our system. It can manifest itself in serious health problems.

Blowing up doesn't seem a very effective strategy either. It is true that by doing so, we release the energy of the emotion and avoid having it trapped inside us, but in most cases the explosion is not productive and can be triggered by trivial circumstances: we end up attacking a waiter only because he took too long to bring us the bill. The explosion can also be counterproductive if it is about euphoria or depression. The exaggerated, uncontrolled expression of an emotion can frighten and embarrass the people around us and have a negative effect on our relationships.

Between the two extremes of suppressing and exploding there is a path that allows us to release the energy that emotions accumulate and use it to get what we want in life.

We live in a society that has taught us that emotions should be hidden, we should be afraid of them or we should be ashamed of them. Despite this we were born with them and every emotion plays an important role in our life. There are no positive or negative emotions, there are only signals that tell the body how to act in any given environment and circumstance. Recognizing these signals, releasing their energy and using it to our advantage, is crucial to having full mastery of our lives.

EMOTION AND TEMPERAMENT

The distinction we need to make at this point is between emotion and temperament. An emotion is a signal activated in the body that may result in changes in the internal climate by which we perceive the feelings associated with it. The emotion has a limited timeframe, meaning it is active in a given situation, and allows us to better respond to external stimuli.

The temperament, in contrast, is an underlying mood based on a dominant feeling that colors our attitudes regardless of external events.

If I am conducting a business negotiation, the emotion of suspicion could help me see which of the conditions my counterpart is including in the contract may damage me.

After it has fulfilled its function, when I have identified the potential danger and adopted a behavior that protects me (for example, requesting to change the terms), I come back to the relationship with the same serenity and confidence that I have always had.

If I have a suspicious temperament, however, I am in a constant state of alert for possible cheating or deception from practically anyone. I see the dark side of any event, I cannot trust those around me.

The temperament, like our emotional responses, was built as a protection against something we feared or suffered from in the past. For example, a very smart colleague of mine has an optimistic temperament. He is always cheerful, never grumpy, always ready with a joke, a person everybody likes to have around.

But when anger turns on, it's as if he is not able to feel it. In the past, there seemed to be nothing that made him angry. When challenged to "feel" anger, he intellectualized in order to avoid it. With a subsequent process of awareness he realized that he had created the strategy of the "cheerful child" in order to compete with his brothers and win

●●●

"Anyone can become angry - that is easy, but to be angry with the right person at the right time, and for the right purpose and in the right way - that is not within everyone's power and that is not easy."
Aristotle.

●●●

the love of the parents, and he unconsciously continued to use this strategy in all aspects of his adult life. From a certain point of view this temperament was functional for him: he developed an incredible ability to connect with others and in his work this allowed him to immediately have good relationships with customers and build up important contacts to develop his business.

From another point of view, when expressing anger may be useful to get something done or to defend himself or others, he fails to take advantage of it.

Reflect on your most frequent emotions and consider whether you have developed a temperament that has been useful in protecting you or in increasing the chance that your needs will be met. Consider the possibility that this temperament may be outdated.

The interesting thing is that no one can change the emotions we feel. We tend to be victims and expect others to make us feel good, and we ask them to behave in a certain way to make us happy. Actually this is pure illusion. Only you can change the emotions you feel. Only you can decide how you prefer to color your days. It's up to you to choose shame, boredom, loneliness, resentment - or joy and love.

EMOTIONAL INTELLIGENCE

The concept of emotional intelligence, already partially introduced by Howard Gardner's theory of multiple intelligences[18], was developed and made

---

[18] The theory of multiple intelligences was formulated by Howard Gardner in 1983 as a model of intelligence differentiated by several specific modalities instead of being dominated by a single ability. Gardner's intelligences are: Musical – Rhythmic, Visual – Spatial, Verbal – Linguistic, Logical – Mathematical, Bodily – Kinesthetic, Interpersonal, Intrapersonal, Naturalistic, Existential

famous by Daniel Goleman. Emotional intelligence (E.I.) involves good management of one's own and others' emotions, without either denying or being overwhelmed by them. It involves two areas, intrapersonal and interpersonal (or social), each with specific skills:

- *intrapersonal skills*: self-awareness, awareness of our moods and feelings, our drivers, and the ability to self-motivate and manage our mental and emotional states even under stress
- *social or interpersonal skills*: understanding others and their feelings, and an ability to interact with them effectively.

Over the past two decades a number of studies have been conducted to identify the effects and the importance of a developed emotional intelligence, and many of them have shown that emotional intelligence and leadership skills are closely linked.
A study by the Center for Creative Leadership (CCL) entitled "The MacIndoe Executive Derailment Study", conducted in the 80s and 90s by the founder of CCL Gail McIndoe, for example, has shown that the main cause of the turnover of managers is linked to a lack of emotional competence. It is mainly about difficulties in the management of change, inability to deal with teamwork, and inadequacy in interpersonal relationships.
In a large company producing beverages, where traditional methods of recruitment of directors of division were adopted, 50% of those recruited left within two years, mainly because of unsatisfactory performance. When the company began to select personnel based on emotional competencies such as initiative, self-confidence and leadership ability, only 6% turnover was recorded. Furthermore, most of the executives whose selection was based on

emotional expertise (87%) reached a performance worthy of high-end productivity awards in their respective divisions.
In more complex tasks (sales people of insurance companies, account managers), a top performer is 127% more productive than an average performer[19] . Research on performance conducted in two hundred companies and organizations around the world suggests that about one third of the difference between a top performer and an average performer is due to cognitive and technical skills, while two-thirds is due to emotional competence. In high-level leadership positions, over 4/5 of the difference is due to emotional competence (Goleman, 1998).
In short, when we are hired what probably matters most is the intelligence quotient (I.Q.), but if we want to be promoted and become a successful manager we must demonstrate emotional intelligence (I.E.).
The good news is that, according to Goleman, emotional intelligence can be developed through proper training, primarily aimed at understanding feelings and emotions, ours and others, and at directing them in a constructive way. While the intelligence linked to the intelligence quotient (IQ) tends to stabilize at around the age of 16 and then begins to decline slowly, we can develop Emotional intelligence throughout the whole course of our life.
The Emotional Intelligence competences can be summarized in *Figure 5-2.*

---

[19] J.E. Hunter, F.L. Schmidt, M.K. Judiesch, “Individual Differences in Output Variabiity As A Function of Job Complexity”, *Journal of Applied Psychology*, 75, 1990, pp 28-42

Figure 5-2 Competences of Emotional Intelligence

SELF AWARENESS

Recognizing our own emotions and their impact:

☐ Knowing what emotions are felt and why
☐ Recognizing the links between one's own feelings and what one thinks, says, does
☐ Being aware of one's own strengths and weaknesses
☐ Knowing one's own value and being confident about one's own skills

SELF MASTERY

Managing emotions and destructive impulses:

☐ Managing one's own uncontrolled feelings and upsets
☐ Being flexible, being able to manage different requests, modifying one's own priorities and change rapidly
☐ Taking responsibility for one's own emotions and personal performance

SELF MOTIVATION

Ability to commit to reach one's own objectives, with energy and enthusiasm:

☐ Being result-oriented
☐ Acting promptly in the face of opportunities
☐ Being led by one's own standards of excellence
☐ Mobilizing others with spirit of initiative

EMPATHY

Ability to tune in to others' emotions and needs and interact appropriately with others:

☐ Understanding others' emotions and points of view
☐ Anticipating, recognizing and meeting the needs of others
☐ Being able to interpret moods and expectations of groups

MANAGING OTHERS' EMOTIONS

Ability to influence groups through common aspirations and goals and building a network of relationships:

☐ Generating enthusiasm toward a common vision and goal
☐ Keeping an effective network of relationships
☐ Facing critical problems with candor and honesty
☐ Listening carefully, looking for mutual understanding, and encouraging information sharing

EXERCISE: YOUR EMOTIONAL COMPETENCE

Try to read the skills related to Emotional Intelligence and identify the three in which you acknowledge you have more talent and the three you have yet to fully develop. I also suggest you ask for feedback from someone who knows you well. Give this observer the list in *Figure 5.2* and ask them to identify the three skills in which you are already strong, and the three that need development. This way you can compare your self-perception with that of others. Often this allows you to discover an interesting discrepancy between what you believe you show and what others see.

COACHING QUESTIONS

With which emotions are you most comfortable?

____

____

____

Which emotions do you find it most difficult to have access to?

____

____

____

What is your usual temperament?

____

____

____

How is anger useful to you? And how is sadness useful to you?

____

____

____

Which emotional intelligence skills would be most beneficial for you to develop to help you achieve your goals?

____

____

____

Part III: Personal Transformation

6. Our Evolutionary Path

IS EVOLUTION ALL A MATTER OF GENES?

With the discovery of DNA, science showed us that DNA genetically determines the human being, that is, genes "control" biology. This resulted in a belief that had a profound effect on the way we have thought about our life and what determines it. Genes represented the best excuse for all kinds of bad behavior ("Do not blame me if I flirt with other women ... it's genetic!") and for our temperament ("What can I do? I have a distrusting nature"). However, the latest developments in biology and genetics have mitigated this biological "determinism".

Recent discoveries have opened new perspectives on the role of the cells, the fundamental elements of our existence. These organisms seek environments that support their survival and avoid the hostile ones. They continuously monitor the surrounding environment and, after analyzing the data received, they select the most appropriate response to ensure the maintenance of their lives.

One of the most interesting findings is that the cells have an evolutionary mechanism that allows them to "learn" from the relationship with the surrounding environment; they create a "memory" that lasts in the organism's body and pass the learned information to the daughters-cells they generate.
Furthermore, discoveries from a revolutionary new field of biology, called epigenetics (literally "about genetics") are profoundly changing our understanding of how life is controlled. Over the past fifteen years, epigenetics has determined that the concrete expression of the genes contained in DNA is not rigidly determined at birth. Influences from the environment - including nutrition, stress and emotions - can modify the expression of genes, without changing the structure of DNA, and these changes can be passed on to future generations as well as the DNA[20].
Genes, then, are not our only destiny. What modifies the cells is the environment in which they live. And in the same way people are modified by the environment that surrounds them.
There are other ways in which a cell learns and changes. Cells have the ability to "capture" energy fields in the electromagnetic spectrum that includes light, sound and radio frequencies, thanks to proteins located in the membrane called "receptors". The antennas of these proteins vibrate like a tuning fork. If an energetic vibration in the environment resonates with an antenna of the

---

[20] W. Reik, J. Walter, "Genomic Imprinting: Parental Influence On The Genome", Nature Reviews Genetics, 2, 2001, pp. 21-32. M. Azim Surani, "Reprogramming Of Genome Function Through Epigenetic Inheritance", Nature, November, 2001, pp. 122-128, http://www.nature.com/nature/journal/v414/n6859/full/44122a0.html.

protein, this will alter its electrical charge, causing a change in the form.
If we think of the energy fields that we have so far explored, namely, the zero-point field that is present throughout the universe, and the energy field of the brain and the heart, we can begin to understand that there is a continuous exchange of energy between ourselves, others, and all that surrounds us, as we are non-locally interconnected to everything.
So, you know, we are not victims of our genes, but masters of our destiny, potentially capable of creating lives that abound with love, peace and happiness. We just need to build a path and the tools that will lead us to discover our true, deep, powerful creative ability.

NEUROPLASTICITY AND CHANGE

As a child I was taught at school that from birth to adulthood the brain is "wired", that is it develops a number of neural connections between cells, and these connections remain almost unchanged, and when we get old we progressively lose some. I learned, as was believed at that time, that the brain develops little by little until, at a certain age, it stabilizes - without the possibility of changes in its connections – and then gradually deteriorates.
I thought that I would become like my parents in many habits and behaviors, because I could only use the neural circuits that I had inherited from them.
Neuroscientists now show that this is not true, as the cells of the brain and neural circuits are subject to various changes during their whole life, which may profoundly alter the pattern of neuronal activation. Thanks to new brain scanning technologies, in fact, neuroscientists have shown

that every thought and experience causes our neurons to connect or disconnect in patterns and sequences that are always different.

Human beings have a capability called "neuroplasticity" which enables them to develop new neuronal circuits and literally change the way they think, in response to new knowledge and new experiences. Every time we learn something new, the brain creates synaptic connections to form new neuronal networks. When we use these circuits in new ways, neurons fire up according to new sequences and we re-wire the brain. And this capacity does not decrease with age.

So every thought, everything we learn, every new experience, every reaction, every memory that we process, every emotion that we elaborate has the potential to change us because it can alter the way our brain works.

Neuroplasticity is an innate ability and allows us to learn from what we experience in the external environment, and to transform this learning into a sustainable modification of our actions, our behaviors, our mental processes and our personality, to get to more functional results. Cognitive learning is not enough: we must transfer the learning to our behaviors to create a new experience.

Without neuroplasticity and the ability to create new synaptic connections we would not be able to make changes, we could not evolve, but would be at the sole mercy of our genetically determined attitudes. Neuroplasticity works as a muscle: to develop it we need to train ourselves to change the perceptions we hold of the world around us, change our points of view, change ourselves.

LEARNING AND TRANSFORMATION CYCLE

In the same way as our cells do, we can grow and evolve as human beings.

The idea that we can learn from the environment and transform our fears, needs, feelings, and behaviors that are not relevant or that get in the way of our personal growth, is very powerful.

The transformational impulse toward personal growth is also an inescapable push of our Higher Self (the Transpersonal Self), one of the needs of the Soul, which, as previously mentioned, puts us in situations and circumstances so that we may experiment new learning processes.

Figure 6-1 Learning and Transformation Cycle

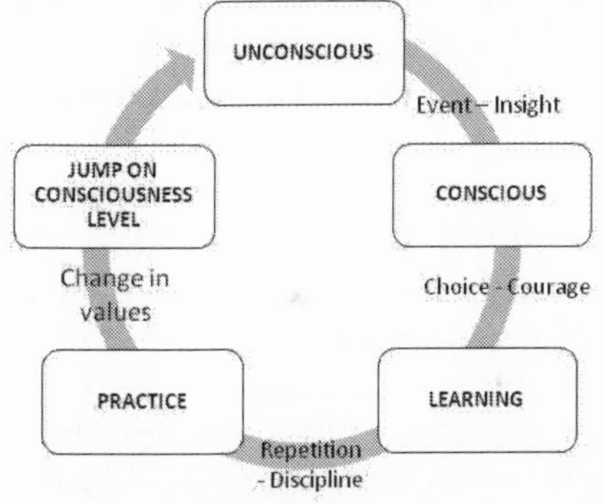

The process of personal evolution is achieved through a cycle of learning and transformation, which uses input from the environment to expand awareness and to encourage changes. Then, through constant practice, the human being includes these changes in a new and expanded behavioral repertoire, until they are ready to embrace a new awareness, and the cycle begins again (*Figure 6.1*).

Let's examine each of the phases. In exploring the cycle I will refer to a personal story that I hope will give you greater clarity of this process.

In the Unconsciousness stage we are simply unaware of a particular limiting aspect of ourselves that is asking to be expanded, managed or overcome. We move forward in life without even realizing it or worrying about this aspect. Sometimes people who are close to us and know us well can see some of our limiting aspects and try to let us know about them, or events happen that could be interpreted in relation to a part of us that asks to grow. When we are not ready to accept this information in our consciousness, we just ignore it and we lose an opportunity for change.
Then something happens (it may be an accident, something we are told, a person who upsets us) and sometimes instantly - as if with a sudden illuminating flash - or sometimes slowly - like a seed that needs time to germinate – it brings us a new awareness, an *insight* about ourselves.
In my personal history, I have always believed myself to be good at communicating my emotions. It never occurred to me that there were some emotions I could not even admit to feeling.
One day, while attending a training course that had to do with emotions, I was asked, as an exercise in sadness, to tell a sad personal story in a way that brought to the surface and communicated how sad I felt. I realized that I was not even able to find appropriate words to tell this story. I was talking in the third person, as if the events had happened to someone else. For me it was like a shock. Suddenly I realized that I had never allowed anyone to get in touch with my sadness, not even myself. Very few people had seen me cry and I had not even cried at the death of my father.
Very often a new awareness emerges from a painful or annoying relationship or event. For example, I always thought that sailing a boat was as simple as windsurfing, which I had done in my

teens. So when a friend, on vacation in a resort, suggested we rent a sailboat together, I immediately accepted. He, too, was unaware of what was involved in piloting a sailboat, and was equipped only with courage and recklessness. When we capsized under the powerful gusts of the mistral and found ourselves in the water, unable to straighten up the boat, climb back on board, and return to shore, I realized that I had no idea of what skills and knowledge I needed to manage that situation.

Sometimes we happen to meet a person who behaves in a way that we can't stand, that bothers us. Meetings of this kind, which at first glance may seem uncomfortable, are a great opportunity for transformation, because these people can reveal a part of us that we have disowned and give us the opportunity to integrate some quality that we have disowned.

Another classic opportunity for insight is when we receive feedback from others. What others perceive of us is a mirror of what we are projecting. We may think that what we are told does not necessarily represent reality, but it is undoubtedly how we are experienced by those around us and, rather than dismiss it, we can use it to expand our self-awareness.

I want to invite you to look back in the past and remember on what occasions you had a sudden realization about yourself or became newly aware of an aspect of yourself that you didn't know about. How did the insight happen, what caused it?

Ultimately, joyful and sorrowful events, the feedback that others give us, or our emotional reactions to life circumstances offer an incredible variety of clues toward greater awareness of ourselves and of those limiting aspects that we have the power to change. But once we have that

awareness - when we know what we did not know before - how can we move forward?
The third step of the cycle is learning. Once I had discovered, on that training course, how difficult it was for me to talk about sadness in my personal history I started to observe my behavior in all the "sad" events of my life and to understand the mechanism underlying the denial of my sadness. I experimented with the way I expressed sadness in front of others and I noticed what was going on for me. I realized that avoiding sadness has always been the strategy to prove to myself and the world that I was strong, self-sufficient and did not need anyone.
A strategy that made up for an unmet need for safety, a mask that covered my fear. And after that I started to open up more, to myself first and to others afterwards, and to share my moments of sadness.
In the case of sailing I decided to enroll on a course and learn the skills I needed to feel confident to handle a boat safely, and when I had developed enough familiarity I got my sailing license.
In both cases, there are two key elements that allowed me to progress from awareness to learning.
The first is *choice*. Once aware of a limited part of me or a skill that I lack, I need to consciously choose to learn the skill or to change the aspect that limits me. I can always choose not to learn to sail a boat or to continue not to show my sadness. The element of *choice* is very important, and often when we fail to learn something it is because, on a subconscious level, we have not made this decision. New Year resolutions are often not followed through precisely for this reason. We have not "chosen" by expressing our full will. Maybe we put them in the list of desired goals because it

would be right, proper, useful to achieve them. But on a deeper level we do not want them.

When I work as an executive coach with managers, part of the coaching contract that I stipulate with the coachee and the sponsors (for example, the boss of the coachee or the human resource manager) is that the objectives of coaching must be "wanted" by the coachee and not imposed on them, so that our work together can bear fruit. We can learn and grow only if we chose to do so and not because we think it is right and logical or if we think we should do it. And even less if others impose it on us.

This aspect of choice is very important. The choice exists as an act of will and the will is the direct expression of the Authentic Self, that inner part that guides us toward growth and the actualization of our potential. To use a metaphor that has been coined by Assagioli, will is like the helmsman of a ship, who sets the new direction that the ship is to follow and keeps it firmly on that course, making the best use of the force (generated by wind, engine or oarsmen) that propels the ship forward. This propulsive energy is completely different from the directional energy of the helmsman who is maneuvering for a change of course.

When we recognize the existence of will, we normally go through a transformative experience, because this opens up possibilities normally denied to those who do not recognize their own will. In this transformative experience we come into contact with a feeling of power and personal responsibility that derives from the possibility of having a certain degree of control over any event, internal or external, that shapes our life.

The second element is *courage*. It takes this ingredient to be able to make a choice to change and learn. Any change, in fact, means leaving the known path and setting out into territories not yet explored. Any change requires us to step out of our comfort zone, the space in which we feel at ease and where we know we can control ourselves and the environment that surrounds us. During my sailboat learning experience I had to use all my courage to put myself at the helm of a 40' boat, put into practice the theoretical lessons I had learned about how to leave a dock without messing up, keep all the variables under control, and open and adjust the sails, in order to have an enjoyable and safe trip.

I was doing things I had never done before and I felt I was not good enough to avoid dangerous mistakes.

Any time we go out of our comfort zone, either because we have decided to do it, or because someone or something has thrown us out against our will, we may feel positive emotions of excitement about the new experience, but mostly we feel fear, loss of control, uncertainty and insecurity.

Sometimes these feelings are so strong that they end up making us abandon what we started and retreat into the comfort and security of what we know. Such feelings of fear have influenced my decision not to try bungee jumping or to learn German. There are learning experiences, for example learning German for me, that we judge to be too extreme or too difficult or not sufficiently useful to face, and so we return to the comfort zone, knowing we haven't given up on something fundamental to our life. However, the risk of spending too much time in our comfort zone is that we fail to experience any new learning.

When we have the courage to acknowledge and face the fears and insecurities that we encounter when we push ourselves outside the comfort zone, then with perseverance and practice we step onto a path of learning and continuous growth. We'll see how we can face our fears in the following chapter. Whenever we integrate a new behavior or a new skill in our repertoire we expand our comfort zone until, at some point, we feel fully comfortable and ready to push forward again to learn something new.

This movement in and out of your comfort zone, the acceptance of the fear and the determination to act in spite of the fear, has made it possible for you to develop as a human being and to learn everything that was needed to get you where you are. It is a natural process of personal evolution.

The fourth phase of the cycle is *practice*. We cannot learn and assimilate any new behavior or skill if we do not practice it constantly for the time needed to allow neurons to strengthen the new synapses that are being generated.

It takes at least 21 days of constant repetition in order to strengthen the connections between neurons linked to the new behavior. Repeating a behavior or action makes it easier and reinforces the new mindset. The great athletes know the power of practice, and they repeat their workouts in order to fully master their sport and prepare themselves for competitions. Musicians also are accustomed to playing their instruments for many hours per day. Practice is the way to learn and internalize experience. When you do a lot of practice, new behaviors or new skills become automatic. We master them so well that we no longer have to focus on them in order to perform.

Have you ever had the feeling, when you are immersed in a particularly fulfilling activity, that while you perform it you almost suspend your thoughts and you can not remember what you did, or that you had been present to what you were doing? This is because repetition leads us to perform tasks with such mastery and concentration that we lose conscious awareness of time and of what we are doing.

This phenomenon is called "being in the flow." When you're in a state of flow you experience a feeling of being highly focused, losing all sense of time, being able to control the activity that you are carrying out without any effort.

Many athletes define the state of flow as the achievement of their best performance while they are at the best of their ability.

The Formula 1 driver Ayrton Senna has described the state of flow in recounting his experience of qualifying for the 1988 Monaco Grand Prix: "I was already in first position, [...] And I was just continuing to go. Suddenly I was nearly two seconds faster than anyone else, including my fellow-pilot with the same car. And I realized that I was no longer driving the car consciously. I'd been driving with a kind of instinct, I was in another dimension. It was as if I was in a tunnel. Not only the tunnel under the hotel but the whole circuit was a tunnel. I went and went, faster and faster and more. I was over the limit but still able to go further."

We need not reach the state of flow in everything we do, but when we want to master an activity, a sport or a behavior, we need to be prepared to have the self-discipline required to practice enough to make it automatic.

When we fully internalize and assimilate the learning, something in the nature of our consciousness profoundly changes and our value system alters. What was important for us yesterday has lost value today and we feel that there are other values emerging.

We integrate a new capacity or new concepts in our awareness and reshape the way we see and experience the world. As if we climbed to a new level of awareness and from there we could see our world through different eyes.

SHIFTING THE ROOT PARADIGM

Usually we use the terms change and transformation as if they were interchangeable. In reality, the meanings of the two words are very different.
If we look in a dictionary, under “change” we would find these definitions:

- substituting something for something else, usually of the same type
- transferring from one to another (for example, "I have to change flight in Milan")
- removing or replacing the cover of something (for example: "The baby's diaper needs to be changed" or "changing the bed")
- becoming altered or modified (for example: "The colors change when they are exposed to the sun")
- leave something for something else ("changing job ")
- exchange

So change, in other words, has to do with a "replacement". We change one thing for another, possibly better or more up-to-date or that works more efficiently. We change a dress, a job, a boyfriend, a diet. We can also change an aspect of our character, but the definitions suggest that change is only on the surface, we haven’t addressed the underlying issue (such as, for example: accepting our body, finding self-motivation and a sense of meaning in anything we do, solving the issue of our emotional dependence, choosing a healthy diet, transcending our need for approval).

Change also appears to be reversible. When I want to go back to the previous state I can do it at any time. On many occasions, the change may be the right strategy to solve a given problem.

In other cases, however, it isn't enough. Maybe we will encounter the same problem in another situation. Let's take the case of the person who is in conflict with a despotic boss. He decides to change job, but after some time he encounters yet another despotic boss or a colleague who creates the same problems. When we respond to the challenges that life offers us with the same change pattern, and the problem keeps coming back, maybe it's time to stop changing and start to consider which part of us wants to undergo a transformation.

Let's have a look at what the most popular dictionaries say on the subject of transformation. We will find these definitions:

- change in form, appearance, nature or character
- change in shape or condition
- metamorphosis
- any change in an organism which alters its character or way of life, such when the larva becomes an insect
- transmutation
- a change in disposition or character

Transformation seems to be a profound and irreversible change in the form or character of an organism. Let's think about what we learned at school about the process of metamorphosis.

The tadpole is completely different in form and function from the frog that it will become. It lives exclusively in the pond with a very limited perspective and experience of the world. It breathes through gills, like a fish. When it turns into a frog, its vision of the world expands: it can jump out of the pond, away from it. But if it wishes it can come back and stay in the water for a while, so it doesn't completely lose its old abilities but instead it integrates them with new and evolving ones. The frog breathes using lungs, its internal organs have changed so that it can adapt to a completely new environment.

The caterpillar has a limited view of the world as well. It crawls on its leaf very slowly. When the metamorphosis takes place, the butterfly can fly high in the sky and see the world from a new and wider perspective. Its body has completely changed and now it can do things that previously it could not even dream of.

Both of these processes are irreversible: the organisms cannot go back to the way they were. In both processes the creatures evolve, undergoing an expansion of their possibilities that are inherent to them. The transformational ability is in their DNA, just as there is a transformational ability in us as human beings. We can become the best we can be and fully express our potential. It is part of our nature. And although transformation is an experience that seems to scare us, we have all experienced it many times in our lives.

Transformation, for us as human beings, is equivalent to a change in the structure of our consciousness, that is, the way in which we think and act. It profoundly alters the root paradigm with which we filter reality, judge and justify it, give meaning to our perceptions, and respond to ourselves, to others and to life circumstances.

This alteration is part of an evolutionary process in which we do not throw away our old skills (which we can always access) but we integrate them with new ones. It is a process that expands our awareness and our repertoire of effective behaviors. And we cannot go back. Once we make a transformation our consciousness expands, the process is irreversible.

Until I was 25, for example, I always looked at nature as an element in which we live and that we can (and must) manipulate to improve the quality of our lives. The land and everything that's in it is separated from me, and it is an inexhaustible source of wealth I can plunder, and that must serve humankind. The values associated with this type of thinking are those related to the power of the human being, utilitarianism, individualism.

One summer my best friend and I had decided to spend the holidays in the Southern United States. The idea was to rent a car and drive from coast to coast. My friend had to pull out at the last minute and I decided to go anyway, making some changes and reducing the itinerary.

It was the first time I had been on holiday alone so far from home. The departure city was Las Vegas and I drove between Nevada and Arizona through the Grand Canyon, Lake Powell, the Petrified Forest, Monument Valley, and Canyon de Chelly on the Navajo Reserve. I didn't know why I had chosen this itinerary, I thought I was fascinated by the history of the Native Americans. On the way from Las Vegas to the Grand Canyon I decided to stop in Sedona, because I had heard it was as a place with a particular energy surrounded by beautiful nature, with high mountains that took on a red color at dusk and dawn. I arrived when it was already dark and I went to bed very early. At 4am I was awake and I decided to take the car and go to see the sunrise on the top of one of the mountains around the city. If I think about it today, I must have been crazy to drive the car in the middle of the night and venture out alone on the trails that lead from the 1,400 meter high city of Sedona up to over 2,000 meters. At dawn, I left the car (a rental car without four-wheel drive which was not suited to this type of ground) and after a short walk I reached the edge of a precipice from which I could see the whole landscape and the reddish reflections of the rocky mountains around me.

I remained silent for a very long time, completely enraptured, to admire that wonder. I think I sat there more than a couple of hours in ecstasy. It was as if what I saw entered in all my senses at once, even with my eyes closed. I cannot explain what happened. Suddenly I felt part of those mountains, of that perfection. It was as if I realized that there was no separation between me and the earth, those rocks, those squirrels.

It was as if I had finally realized that there was something more to discover about myself and about the nature of human beings, and I had the distinct feeling of a greater meaning in my life. Slowly, after that experience, I started to make a series of decisions that directed my life toward a greater awareness and to the values of unity, service to others, personal growth. The experience of Sedona was a real shift in my root paradigm: moving from nature as an object to be exploited to the unity of all things and thus Nature as part of myself.

We have a common experience of transformation of our root paradigm, at least in most cases, when we become parents. Suddenly we "know" that we are no longer kids and we develop a different view of ourselves. Transformations of the root paradigm don't always arrive because of an experience of beauty and grace.

Very often they are generated by moments of pain or extreme discomfort. When I was twelve I witnessed my father falling from his horse and I was at his side during the year of rehabilitation, at the end of which he still hadn't recovered the full use of his legs and organs from the waist down.

After that event my vision of myself was reversed from that of a spoiled child, to whom everything is due, to an active and responsible member of the family, who contributed to its functioning and to the care required to keep it emotionally stable. It was a real 180 degrees change in my life. And it was irreversible, a true metamorphosis.

This transformation of the paradigm is a natural process of development and growth. It is also an integrative process, in which we connect new capabilities to our existing wealth of experience and ability. It is an expansive process, because it expands our point of view, the ways in which we manage ourselves and events. And it is an evolutionary process, because it raises our awareness in a way that enables us to manage increasingly complex situations.

Transformations happen to everybody, you've already experienced them several times in your life. Maybe you never stopped to think about and appreciate this process of growth that allowed you to get to where you are today. With greater mastery, however, you can stimulate it when it is useful for you to continue to grow and to develop.

Try to remember those moments in life when you experienced a transformation of your root paradigm, when you saw yourself or your circumstances in a radically different way from before. Review those moments. Stop reading the book for a few minutes, close your eyes and go back to situations that have resulted in a profound irreversible change.

Reflect on these experiences: what happened, how did you live the events, and how have they transformed your root paradigm?

EXERCISE: THE TRANSFORMATIONS IN YOUR LIFE

What event preceded the transformation of your root paradigm? (eg, a loss, you left your family and lived alone, an accident etc..). Describe what happened in detail.

____

____

What did you feel?

____

____

What impact did this have on you? How did your root paradigm change?

____

____

COACHING QUESTIONS

When have you experienced a shift in your root paradigms in your life?

____

____

____

What experiences or events provided you with a new awareness, made you realize something that you didn't know before?

____

____

____

Can you find a pattern in these experiences, elements that keep recurring?

____

____

____

In which areas did you tend to stay in your comfort zone? Which paradigms have you never questioned?

____

____

____

What hinders your path of growth, in your experience?

____

____

____

7. Fears and Other Brakes

WHAT GETS IN THE WAY OF TRANSFORMATION

We all have the power to transform our thoughts, our emotions, and our paradigms. But we don't always do that. It is easier in specific events such as a big accident, a moment of enlightenment, an illness, a major life change. The transformational ability, however, requires a certain willingness to see the opportunities for growth and transformation also in "trivial" events: a discussion with a colleague, a comment that you receive from a friend or a relative, or one of your idiosyncrasies.

Transformation, we have seen, requires a choice. Everyone has the opportunity to move toward personal fulfillment and take responsibility for the degree of evolution and awareness achieved. Each of us can choose whether to simply carry out our biological functions, to exist according to a program built up during millions of generations, or to look beyond the borders of our own maps – for a greater degree of awareness to determine the course of

our lives and stop living on autopilot which makes the choices on our behalf. This is not an issue of merit; there isn't a difference in moral value between the possibilities we decide to pursue. It is only a personal choice that impacts our life.
If you decide to set sail for new unknown lands, you will face insidious seas and challenges, with no certainty of what you'll find. You are not be better or worse than others who choose to stay in the already explored territories. Everyone will reap the fruits of their own quest. The better the result meets the expectations, the more it will be appreciated.
Each of us - whether we are aware of it or not - makes the difference, makes choices (not choosing is a choice as well) and experiences all the consequences.
It does not matter which place we start from, what system of paradigms we have, which map of the world we inherited from the previous generation. Whatever the point of departure, we make a difference and on this difference we can measure the miles we walked. We may look back with satisfaction, still finding new reasons to continue our journey.
Very often, even if we do not realize it, we tend to avoid the transformation, to react even aggressively in order not to question what we believe in, the way we conduct ourselves, our personality. We prefer not to question our paradigms, so as to avoid the anxiety and continue to feel at ease in our comfort zone.
Here we feel safe, we are able to manage whatever we encounter, we experience a sense of control, satisfaction, serenity, relaxation, although sometimes we feel bored because we find little excitement.
Beyond the comfort zone there is a new paradigm, a quest that we might choose to undertake, an

emergent way of thinking that could open up new windows and new opportunities.

To be able to move outside the comfort zone, in an area we can call the learning zone, we must go through a transition zone, a boundary where our fears lurk, where we no longer have contact with that place that makes us feel safe, but where we have not yet reached the final destination. It's like being a trapeze artist who is hanging from the swinging bar and sees another bar in front of him, where he knows he will meet his growth. He understands he must jump to reach it. But there is a moment when, in the jump, he is suspended in the void between what he has left and what he will find. It is in that space that the transformation happens. And it takes all his courage.

Fear is the main obstacle to our growth. When we start a new business, develop a new competence or behavior, we potentially put our self-confidence at risk. We risk making a bad impression, losing power, appearing silly or being rejected, feeling humiliated or insecure. Whatever it is we fear, we risk encountering it. It is important to acknowledge our fears, in order to be aware that what we fear is not reality, but it is only a story we tell ourselves, which is based on our past and on the needs at the bottom of our iceberg.

Let's take an example. You have just been promoted in a new role and your former peers are now your subordinates. Month after month you notice that one of them is not performing as he should and you know that the company expects a decisive action from you to put the guy back on track.

You would like to give him timely feedback and demand more attention from him, but you're afraid to ruin the relationship of camaraderie that was established when you were just colleagues. On various occasions, since you were a child, the voice of your "inner critic" has repeated: "If you tell the truth, others will not want to be around you anymore." You have heard it so many times that for you it has become a reality: truth = rejection. Every time you try to give honest feedback, you believe that the relationship will be ruined. In this case you have internalized the fear of rejection so much that you do not even recognize it as a fear. This is a most serious situation, because not only is your fear getting in the way of the achievement of your goals, but you do not even recognize it, or realize its impact on you.

Acknowledging your fear is the first step to seeing it for what it is, and considering it as an object, a story that you have created in the past and you have never before questioned. Always look for the reasons why you don't do a certain thing.

Fear is also what blocks change initiatives in organizations. Change initiatives are often initially launched with great enthusiasm and then they gradually reveal themselves as more complex than expected.

For years in business literature we have been reading about "change management" as a structured approach to change. Change in an organization is, on one hand, about the organizational structure, processes and technologies, and on the other, about the people who must adapt to the change, or are even expected to generate it. Unfortunately, most of the change initiatives in organizations are not destined to reach their full potential, or they fail altogether. The reason for the failure is people's fear, their innate drive to stay in the area of comfort and therefore to maintain the status quo. The fear of change in people (and the lack of familiarity of

managers with helping their employees to cope with change) sets up the initiative for failure.
A change, even as simple as the replacement of an old technological platform with a new one, requires people to abandon the way of working in which they feel at ease, for a new way they still need to learn and that makes them feel insecure, uncertain. The most natural reaction to change is fear, which materializes in resistance and that unfolds in open ways (hostility, aggression, rejection) or in more subtle ways (apparent openness but subsequent "inaction", sabotage, forgetfulness).
In organizations, leaders erroneously believe that once the change is implemented and communicated to the managers (for example a new technological platform or a reorganization), people will automatically adapt to the new reality. This is rarely the case. Organizations do not change. It's only people who can create a change in the collective root paradigm and make the organization change, through a transformation in the way they see themselves and their work. Otherwise, like the monkeys we met in *Chapter 1*, they will tend to avoid the ladder to get the banana.
Shedding light on what prevents us from making a change is very important if we are to identify the ways in which we sabotage ourselves and in general to learn when and how our fear emerges, to be able to manage it with greater effectiveness.

A PERSONALITY CREATED TO AVOID SUFFERING

When we are born we are unable to survive on our own. We need unconditional love and protection. We also need to be considered, seen. When these needs are met, our experience of the world is positive, full of confidence, and we can express our true nature of joy and love. We are curious to know the world around us, which responds by offering us little challenges that make us learn to manage ourselves and what is outside of us.

When we are children we do not have the concept of time. For us there is no past and future. We live only in the present moment. I look at my three year old great-nephew. He builds and destroys constructions of colored bricks and nothing in the world can be more interesting to him than what he is doing right now. I can call him, invite him to play something else, but I do not get any response. A few minutes later he becomes angry because the cat has moved the bricks and nothing is more important for him than what the cat has just done. He begins to cry in anger at the cat and seems desperate, tears rolling down his cheeks, and there is no way of comforting him. A moment later he notices something sticking out from underneath the couch and immediately gets his smile back and goes exploring the strange thing. The bricks are forgotten, as well as the cat, the anger and the crying.

As children, we have an incredible ability to feel our emotions, to live them. We may not be able to contain them, but we express what goes on inside us without filters. We are completely authentic. Filter-free, we begin to "download " messages from our parents. Even before knowing the verbal language, we are very good at "reading" the emotions and reactions of adults, at deciphering their meanings and consequences for us, and at understanding what makes adults happy or unhappy. Many of us also begin to experience difficulties and suffer from them. We may feel abandoned and in danger of death if we remain separated from our mothers. For a child a brief absence or actual neglect are the same thing. As we have said, up to 18 months we only live in the present and a minute or ten days seem the same. We may feel rejected if our parents respond indifferently to our effusions, if they don't hug us and smile at us.

We begin to observe what our parents do and we store these behaviors. We store their emotions as well. In fact, our mirror neurons allow us to be attuned to the emotions felt by those around us and in particular to those of the mother.

At that age, among other things, we cannot tell the difference between our own emotions and those felt by our mother. The emotional climate that we experience in the family (or our reaction to it) can then be transformed into a further aspect of our temperament.

Through experience and observation, we learn how to cope with our emotions. When the experience is painful, we learn to react with fear-based protective patterns, that manifest themselves as the "fight, flight, freeze" behaviors. We store both our responses and our reactions in the neuronal system, associating them with the type of event that triggers them.

Between 2 and 4, we begin to develop the part of the brain called "limbic brain" and the ability to verbalize what we think and how we feel. We can give a name to objects around us and begin to listen and learn from adults and other people around us who we are or who we should be (and are not). We are young and we trust in what mom and dad tell us. We have to believe it, otherwise how would we survive? And if they say that we are beautiful we believe it, but we believe it even when they say we're stupid, we're bad, we're worthless. We also understand what we are lacking that would make us worthy of love. We understand that if we are not obedient we will be punished, that if we do not do what our parents ask us they will call the Candyman or policeman to take us away, or other equivalent threats. Here is how our primary need, the need for unconditional love, remains for most of us unmet. We learn that we cannot be loved as who we are, but we will be loved only under certain conditions.

The fear of not being loved unconditionally can dominate us for a lifetime. When we are children, we need our parents and therefore we do not even realize that we are undergoing enormous stress. Many children, abused physically or psychologically, remove the cause of the stress from their memories, but the body and the subconscious mind don't forget. In later years we may discover we have buried these memories so effectively that we're pretty sure we were raised in the best way, and remember only a happy childhood.

As we acquire language we also start to assimilate the paradigms of our family and our culture, as if they were truth when they are, in fact, only paradigms that have never been questioned. "Real men don't cry", "A woman can only be fulfilled when she's financially independent," "The world is dangerous", "Money is dirty" and so on. Little by little, tracks on the imaginary DVD of our brain are formed and are reinforced by repetition.

Then we start to build our paradigms, so as to feel safe. We begin to form our iceberg and develop values, thoughts, emotions and behaviors associated with all the positive and negative experiences, including those in which our unmet needs in childhood or in later years keep being unfulfilled.

We fear, for example, that we won't be appreciated, that we are not worthy. Career and professional success can become values to which we incessantly devote our time, and we try hard to show in every possible way that we meet expectations, that we are winners. We accept yet another project that will keep us away from our family, convinced it's because we love our work, and actually act compulsively in the hope of finally being admired in the future. We operate in a competitive way and we depend on our results to convince us that we are worthy.

Or we learned that in order to be loved we need to be perfect. Trying to be perfect is a hard job: I speak from experience. We develop values related to precision and accuracy, and we try to keep ourselves and the environment under control to ensure the final result. We become unbearable parents and leaders because in order to be perfect we need others to be imperfect. We judge what others do, which is never how we would do it, and we reduce to a state of exhaustion anyone working with us with our mania of control.

Or again our unmet need of unconditional love can make us particularly careful to put the needs of others before ourselves, because if we can make others happy, then perhaps we will be loved. The values of generosity and reliability become important to us and we put ourselves tirelessly in the service of others, in work or in relationships, without realizing that we are not respecting ourselves.

Our values, what is really important to us, are likely to be the justification of our dysfunctional behaviors as well as the functional ones. In fact, if we are too anxious to keep our freedom in a relationship and justify our unavailability by appealing to our value of independence, we should ask ourselves if by any chance this does not serve as a protection from the risk of abandonment or rejection: I give value to

independence, so I will not fully commit, therefore I will not be abandoned.
The stronger we hold a value, the more we are ready to defend it tooth and nail, the greater the possibility that it was developed as a means of protection to prevent the umpteenth unmet need. Exploring our own values is another way of discovering our iceberg. If you want, go back to the section on *The nature of our behavior* and try to do the iceberg exercise starting from your values (from page 59).
Mind you, I am not saying that it's not nice to achieve results in our own work or that we as managers should not control our employees, that we should not help others, or that we should not keep some kind of independence.
I'm just saying that when these activities are guided by a protection mechanism which is stronger than us and we cannot calibrate and manage them, then we become slaves to them and our behavior will be directed only to the satisfaction of the need. Let me give an example: if I call a friend to go to a movie and she says she cannot come because she has another commitment, I may be sorry, but I would not attach much importance to it. If instead my unmet need is to be considered and so I'm afraid of any rejection, I might not risk calling my friend for fear of receiving the fateful "No, thank you."
These are just a few examples. The unmet needs of children, over the years, develop and follow their own circuitous paths, according to experiences, and diverge into many types of need.
Of course all of our unmet needs can be traced back to one of the four basic needs with which we are born. They will make us develop paradigms that have the function of rationalizing our behavior and justifing them, in addition to putting a reactive

defense system in place to protect us at a physical and emotional level.

To make sure all the apparatus functions, we must also believe that the satisfaction of our needs comes from the outside and that others have to carry this burden. So it must be our husband/wife, our boss or our parents who are to make us feel appreciated. The behaviors of others will make us feel loved, safe, valued, recognized, listened to, and so on. When this does not happen it is because others "have done something to us". We act as victims: our well-being, our happiness, our balance, our confidence, all depends on others. If things do not go as we want it is not our responsibility. If we feel bad it is somebody else's fault. If we do not get the promotion it's because the boss turned against us. If we are not happy it is because our spouse does not love us enough, and so on.

What we must always remember is that all of this apparatus - paradigms and reactive protection systems - consists of layers, like an onion, in which we wrap ourselves for protection, but in the long run they end up becoming walls that hide our true nature, our personal self, our authenticity, our innate joy from ourselves and from others and force us into a cage. A cage to which we become so accustomed that we don't notice it anymore.

What we call our personality is nothing but our shield. Under the armor, there is still the wonderful, perfect, lovable being we were when we were born. Only the armor is so thick and strong, and feeling "naked" scares us so much, that we convince ourselves we are the armor, not the being inside.

When we build a way of being and acting based on avoiding pain, we provide others with a tool to get what they want from us. The protection mechanisms that we activate, and that we have difficulty in recognizing, are indeed immediately perceived by those around us. It is like living with a switch panel on the back. We do not see it, but others do and they can press a button to trigger a predictable response.

For example, if we carry the unmet need of recognition, and we want to discuss with the boss a salary increase, we may find ourselves receiving many compliments that will make us feel so appreciated that we don't even react to the "no" that the boss slips into the conversation.

And we'll leave his office feeling content. Children are very good at pressing the mother's buttons. If mom lives with the unmet need to be needed, her son will easily manipulate her using phrases like "If I didn't have you..." to get his mountain of clothes ironed.

The more we try to avoid suffering, the more we make our panel visible and we prepare ourselves to be more easily manipulated. Without realizing it, we create the strings to which we link ourselves and put them at the disposal of those who will become our puppeteers.

A MODEL FOR UNDERSTANDING OUR FEARS

There are many psychologists and philosophers who have explored fear in the context of the path of development of the human being.

Certainly among the most important contributors is Fritz Riemann[21]. The work of these scholars allows us to have a deeper understanding of the four basic fears and the polarity within which we operate.

---

[21] Fritz Riemann, *Anxiety. Using Depth Psychology to Find a Balance in Your Life*, Ernst Reinhardt, Munich/Basel, 2008

In *Chapter 2*, we learned that we are born with two pairs of psychological needs that are opposites of each other:

1. love (or belonging to someone, to a group) and
2. self-expression, independence
3. safety, predictability and
4. variety, unpredictability

There are four fears connected with the possibility that these needs remain unsatisfied. They are organized along two axes (see *Figure 7.1*), which represent two fundamental themes in our lives. These are the (horizontal) affiliation axis and the (vertical) control axis:

1. being alone, separation
2. feeling suffocated by others
3. lack of control
4. boredom, feeling trapped

In order to feel complete and balanced, all our needs must be met. This satisfaction can be difficult, because these four energies are by nature contradictory.

Figure 7-1 The four fears

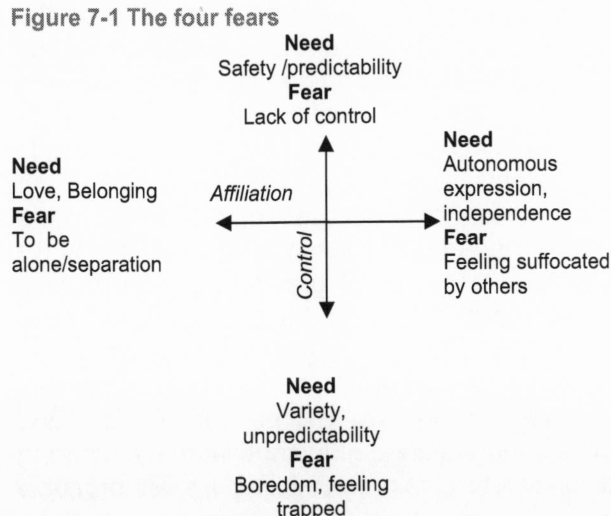

On one hand we have to become mature individuals, able to accept our independence and to differentiate ourselves from others (self-expression need). On the other hand we must trust life, the world and people, let others get close to us and be available to create intimacy with others (need of belonging and love).
On the one hand, we should achieve consistency and certainty, develop plans and follow them in a predictable way (safety and predictability need). At the same time, we should remain flexible, open to change, willing to embrace the unknown and abandon what we know.
As we grow older, we often experience having to sacrifice the satisfaction of one need in favor of another. In some families, parents encourage their children to express all of these needs. In others, unfortunately most of them, the child discovers that she will not get the satisfaction of a need if she expresses its opposite. For example, in many families, children learn that self-expression (wanting to be independent or seeking to assert their opinions even if different from that of the parents) can compromise the satisfaction of the need for love and belonging. In other cases the child learns that the expression of a need is beneficial because it ensures the love and attention of their parents.
In the process of socialization, the focus on a particular need ensures survival, and that's why we start to form a center of gravity around it from a very early age. When we have a particular focus on a need, we develop a series of talents around it. For example, if we have a strong need for variety and unpredictability, we will be very flexible and effective during change. If instead we have a strong need for safety and predictability, we will probably

be good planners. When we feel the satisfaction of a need is in danger in any way, then the corresponding fear is triggered, which gives rise to a typical reactive response that quickly becomes dysfunctional for ourselves and for others.
To better understand the correlation between each need and its relative fear, let's examine the four types of fears we mentioned before, one by one.

1. Fear of being alone, separation

People who have a strong inclination toward the need of love and belonging need to create closeness and connection with others. This need is connected to the desire to be part of a group, to share and feel our own worth acknowledged by others, to make others happy.
These people are very effective in teamwork, are participatory, and are those who mediate in conflicts. They love friendliness and loyalty. They like to feel connected to others, to their bosses or to colleagues or to their sports group: they feel these bonds and these connections as a source of personal harmony and safety. They tend to create dependent relationships: they feel dependent on others and attempt, with their behavior, to make others dependent on them.
The stronger fear is being rejected, abandoned, set aside with respect to a person or a group. Separation from others means being alone and independent, a status from which they flee to the point of foregoing themselves. In relationships this leads to an inability to see potentially challenging situations, not wanting to clarify what has been withheld, for fear of creating tensions with others. In organizations these people find it very difficult to give constructive feedback or to conduct performance assessments.

Any time criticism is called for, they dilute or sugarcoat potentially negative messages to avoid affecting the harmony in the relationship or putting group membership at risk.
As a result of their fear of separation or abandonment, these people tend to sacrifice time, resources and energy to others, to idealize the context in which they live, and not to question individuals or groups with whom they want to maintain a connection. They often read between the lines of anything they are told, to look for signs that may alert them to any dissatisfaction or potential withdrawal. The greatest fear relates to their individuation and autonomy, because these are perceived as achievable only in association with isolation and loss of protection.

2. Fear of being suffocated by others

The opposite to those in need of love and belonging, we find those who have the need to assert their individual Self, their independence, their freedom. These people want to be able to decide for themselves, to have their own opinions and express them even if in opposition to others, they don't want to depend on anyone and they constantly set boundaries to what they allow others to do or to tell them.
They know how to defend their ideas and make difficult decisions. They develop their own sense of discernment and judgment with which they evaluate others and circumstances. They can be excellent negotiators or analysts.
They protect their own space and keep people at a safe distance.
Sometimes they may seem arrogant. They try not to manifest their emotions, not to "let go" and to remain rational, logical and objective. The manifestation of feelings, love and friendship are all

threats to their identity and they defend themselves from these manifestations sometimes aggressively, sometimes with irony and sarcasm to restore the distance from others.
Their biggest fear is to lose themselves and their autonomy if they give themselves to others.

3. Fear of lack of control

People who have a strong need for certainty and predictability love well-organized contexts, with clear and well defined procedures. They want everything to be under control, optimized and done in obedience to the rules. Their gifts are perfectionism, discipline, organizational skills, compliance and reliability. In organizations they are those who remind everyone "how we do things here" and follow rules and policies with precision.
Anything representing a change or a novelty is unwelcome, because these things feed uncertainty. What is outside their way of doing things is a danger for their safety. They tend to resist change, they do not allow for spontaneity, lose efficiency in situations of transition because of the typical doubts and the uncertainty they experience in times of change or when situations are not clear or structured. They look for a "universal order". They can be very slow decision makers, because they weigh up all the elements with extreme caution and plan every detail before taking a risk.
They tend to hide behind their habits, because every change causes a state of anxiety and they have a resistance to embed new concepts and skills.
Their deepest fear is change because it is experienced as a loss of safety and of those anchors dictated by tradition upon which they base their existence.

4. Fear of boredom, feeling trapped

People who have a strong need for variety and unpredictability are creative and spontaneous individuals. They always look for new ideas and solutions. They have personalities that prefer a sense of adventure and the unexpected rather than the safety of what is known. They may be competitive and want to be admired. They love everything that means novelty, change, unpredictability, or rule-breaking. They are great designers, artists, entrepreneurs, communicators.

Tradition, boundaries, rules and procedures are all elements that limit their freedom, which must be defended at all costs. They encounter difficulties in planning because they always keep different options open, or in following procedures and rules, in systematizing their work. They are reluctant to submit to social conventions because these limit their freedom. You cannot expect punctuality and reliability from these people. Boredom is one of the emotions that they avoid as much as possible. Their relationships need constant renewal, otherwise they feel like prisoners of habit and they run away.

The greatest fear is being trapped and losing their freedom.

FACING OUR FEARS

Fears are a normal part of our lives and none of them are more right or more wrong than others. The problem arises when we deny a fear or when we develop an attachment to one of our needs. All we want is to feel safe, but this means expecting things to remain as we have known and experienced them. The limit is losing the richness of life. But if we consider fears as our friends, every recurring fear can be a warning sign that indicates we're trying to avoid something inevitable, something that life is demanding of us. So, if we can see fears as gifts, we can integrate them and transcend them, becoming more whole and more fully alive.

To be able to integrate our fears, we must first become aware that most of them are based on assumptions we never questioned, but that we accepted as reality.

Figure 7-2 The four fears model

Need
Safety /predictability
Fear
Lack of control
Reactive response
Worrying excessively micro-management
Talent
Reliability, structure

Need
Love, Belonging
Fear
To be alone/separation
Reactive response
Being needy
Talent
Creating connections with others

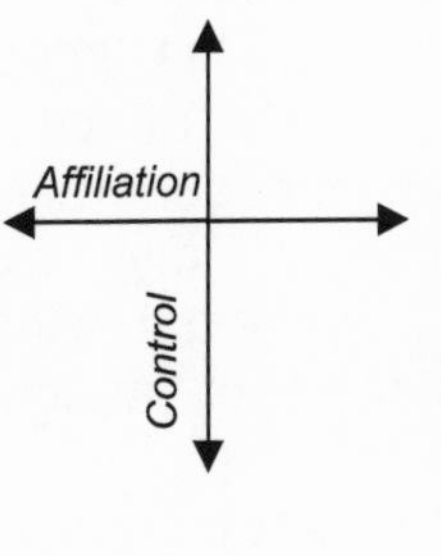

Need
Autonomous expression, independence
Fear
Feeling suffocated by others
Reactive response
Keeping others away, emphasize independence
Talent
Giving autonomy to self and others

Need
Variety, unpredictability
Fear
Boredom, feeling trapped
Reactive response
Resistance, rebellion
Talent
Flexibility, stimulus

7. Fears and Other Brakes

Fear - unless it's triggered in situations of physical danger, such as when we cross a road and a car approaches at high speed, or when we grab a hot object – is generally not about what's happening here and now.

It is most often linked to future events, which by definition have not yet occurred. It is based on the stories we tell ourselves and our beliefs, and not on what is actually happening at the present time.

For example, if my fear is that I cannot count on others because I think they will disappoint me, I'm not considering what is happening at this very moment, but I'm probably basing this assumption on the fact that years ago - maybe even in the early years of my life - somebody I counted on didn't behave as I expected - and I developed the belief that "all" the people I meet will "always" disappoint me.

Whenever we use absolute terms like "always", "never", "every time", "all the time", we take out a mortgage on our future, affecting the way we behave with others, and generating just what we wanted to avoid: in my example, others disappointing me. Think about what you're afraid of and ask if at this moment, at this very moment, you're risking what you fear.

If we can understand that the mechanism of fear is not based on reality, but on a story that we have built as a result of an event that happened in the past, we are doing well. What we need to do now is:

1. identify the needs which give rise to fear, the story or the belief that we tell ourselves around that need
2. question the story or belief
3. develop the qualities of those who have the opposite need

Identify the need and the story we tell ourselves

The first step is to explore our fears and the beliefs we have developed that support them. I will lead you through a process of personal reflection to allow you to explore the roots of your most important fear. Take fifteen minutes of uninterrupted time in a quiet place where you will not be disturbed.

Think about a behavior that you would like very much to develop, but which represents an insurmountable difficulty for you. It must be a behavior that you know would be useful, that would greatly benefit you in your private or professional life (or perhaps in both!) and that requires that you change significantly.

It must be a behavior you aspire to, but that is difficult for you to enact. I will use an example to give you a reference point in your exploration.

Write below the desired behavior:

For example: I would like to say no when my colleagues ask me to help them complete a report.

____

____

Now imagine enacting this desired behavior. What is the worst consequence that could happen? Write the consequence:

For example: They might think they cannot count on me when they need to.

____

____

If this consequence actually came true (in the example described, if your colleagues really thought they cannot count on you), what would be

the worst consequence that could happen? Write the consequence:
For example: they would feel disappointed and stop being as friendly as they normally are.

____

____

If this consequence actually came true (in the example described if your colleagues were really disappointed and not friendly anymore), what would be the worst consequence that could happen? Write the consequence:
For example: I would feel excluded and unwanted.

____

____

If you've had the courage to explore in depth, you may have arrived at a fear that resembles one of the four fears that we described earlier:
1. being alone, separation
2. feeling suffocated by others
3. lack of control
4. boredom, feeling trapped

Do you think you have got to the bottom of this exploration, to the biggest fear? Not yet? Then continue with another question.
If this consequence actually came true, which would be the worst consequence that could happen? Write the consequence:

____

____

In our example, we touched on the underlying fear: the fear of separation, of being abandoned.

Questioning the assumption or story we tell ourselves

One of the most effective ways to create a personal transformation is identifying the story or the assumption we use to support and make fear necessary. These stories or assumptions are only mental constructions, ways that we use to give meaning and to interpret what happens to us, but we treat them as if they were reality, incontrovertible facts. And we are so unaware of it that we are surprised if others do not agree with us. These stories are assumptions, and therefore may be true, but they might not be. And more usually, in fact, they are not. The great advantage of questioning our stories is to turn them from an integral part of us, of our mindset (and therefore invisible to us because we are fully identified with them), into a subject of study and reflection about which we can develop a point of view or perspective, and seeing them "outside" of ourselves.

Reflect on the fear that you've identified. On what basis did you develop it? What do you say to yourself about why you are afraid that what you fear will happen (in the example, why do I believe that I could be excluded)? Try to write down the explanation that you give yourself about the reason the behavior you avoid is dangerous:

____

____

____

If you have difficulty identifying the story you tell yourself about the reason for the fear, try to see if by chance it looks like one of those in the list below.

Fear of being alone, separation

- If I tell the truth (or a bad thing) others will hate me
- I am only ok if others like me
- If I disappoint others, they will not want me anymore
- I have to live up to people's expectations
- I will be appreciated only until I am indispensable
- I'm not good enough

Fear of being suffocated by others

- I cannot trust anyone
- If I were to open up people would hurt me
- I don't need others to feel good
- I am right, it's others who are wrong
- I need to be better than others to feel good
- I feel I am worthy when others look at me with admiration

Fear of lack of control

- Changes are dangerous
- If my life is not well organized I feel insecure
- Failure (of any type) is the end for me
- Procedures and rules are made to be followed
- Better to stick with tried and tested methods
- Exposing myself and my ideas is dangerous

Fear of boredom, feeling trapped

- Habit kills me
- Taking on a commitment means trapping myself
- I need novelty (or to constantly change) just to feel alive
- Rules are made to be broken

You may perceive some of the assumptions you are uncovering as true, while others may not seem necessarily true, and you might feel uncertain about others. Sometimes these assumptions are based on actual experiences you have had in the past. Other times, they are based on things that you've heard or you've imagined but never experienced.

In any case, you will agree that there is no certainty that they will be true in the near future, unless you conduct a proper investigation to understand what the odds are.

The exploration and testing of these assumptions may open the doors to a new world for you, a world you haven't given yourself permission to discover before, a world where you can remove the limits that you unknowingly imposed on yourself and unleash your full potential.

Exploring and testing the assumptions requires you to commit yourself, just like a researcher, to studying and questioning every assumption you've made, as if it were being made by someone else.

There are various ways in which you can test an assumption. One of these you've already discovered in Chapter 4 when you learned to challenge negative thoughts. You can use the same sequence of questions to become aware that assumptions are mental constructions and that you can choose to adopt other ways of seeing reality.

Another method is to use your intellect and your analytical skills to identify the origin of the assumption and the consequences that you create when you believe it.

To test the assumption you can proceed with the analysis of the four aspects that follow.

1. Origins: When did you develop this assumption?

Normally there is a time in our lives when the assumption emerges and we begin to believe it. It

might be because it was always repeated to us by our parents and in the end we believed it. Or because we had an experience as a child or a young adult when our needs went unsatisfied. Or because we saw someone else in danger or punished because of this experience.
At the time we did not have the ability to reflect and give meaning to what happened in a rational and constructive way. We catalogued the experience as dangerous, and we have generalized it.
We therefore took an experience that happened once and, reading the future, we determined that it would always happen. Try to go back in time and identify that key experience that made you develop the assumption.
What happened in your life at that time? Which emotions did you feel? What really scared you?

____

____

____

2. Consequences: if you continue to believe this story or assumption, what consequences do you create?
As we said about the observer-created reality, thoughts we believe affect your view of reality, and your behavior will only generate responses from the environment that will confirm and enhance your paradigm. So the stories that you tell yourself become self-fulfilling prophecies.
Try to investigate what consequences you create through the stories you believe. When you believe your assumption, how do you behave with others?

____

____

____

As a consequence, which reaction do you stimulate in others, that feeds your assumption?

____

____

____

What new behavior could you choose that would radically change the reaction of others?

____

____

____

3. Probability: What are the odds that this assumption will be fulfilled if you adopt the new behavior?

Try a thought experiment. Imagine a situation in which the fear linked to the assumption could snap. Imagine that, instead of reacting as you always have in the past, you manage to adopt the new behavior you just identified. How likely is it that the assumed outcome will occur? (Try to give an assessment as a percentage, where from 0% to 10% means that there is a low or insignificant chance, and from 90% to 100% means it will almost certainly happen).

____

____

____

4. Opposite: can you demonstrate that the opposite is as true as the assumption?
Find as many possible pieces of evidences and examples that demonstrate that the opposite possibility is also true. For example, if your assumption is "If I was in need, no one would help me," you will need to find a few examples in your life of occasions when you received help.

____

____

____

What new knowledge have you gained? What do you know now about yourself that you did not know before? And how can you use these new insights to better deal with your fear?

Develop the qualities of someone who has the opposite need

The third step is to integrate the qualities (talents) of the need opposite to ours. This means choosing to focus on an aspect of ourselves that we want to develop.

We may look at the people who seem to put us in the greatest difficulty as life teachers, because they have access to a quality or talent that we have not yet developed. If you look at *Figure 7.3* again, you'll notice that what we must learn if we are to integrate our fear has to do with the talent of those who have the opposite fear.

To become psychologically mature, we have a responsibility to find our balance in the contradictions that life presents us with, and consciously choose to embrace the need of the profile opposite to ours.

If you are afraid of being alone or being abandoned, the profile opposite to yours is someone with a strong need for autonomous expression. The integration will be learning to become an independent person.
What is present in your life today that could help you move your focus from ensuring that your need of attention or love or membership is constantly satisfied to activating your need for self-expression? Which relationship in your life would be enhanced if you learned to be independent instead of expecting others to make you feel worthy?
If you are afraid of being suffocated by others, you will need to learn to give yourself, to allow yourself to be intimate with someone.
What would be the benefit if, instead of insisting on your autonomy and independence, you focused your energy toward your need to give and receive love? How could your professional life benefit? Which relationship in your life would be renewed as a result?
If you are afraid of losing control, you will need to learn to appreciate change and growth, to let yourself go. What might be possible if you could embrace your need for variety and the unexpected, without worrying about how much uncertainty you will face? What would you make possible in your work that today seems inconceivable? Which relationships would benefit if you quit taking too much responsibility, if you stop wanting to put others in boxes, and instead embrace the more rebellious and wild part of yourself?
If you are afraid of feeling trapped, you will need to learn how to make a commitment, how to accept routine, agreements, rules. Instead of constantly seeking new situations and stimuli, what if you were

able to activate your needs of certainty and stability?

Figure 7-3 Integrating the fears

Need
Safety /predictability
Fear
Lack of control
Reactive response
Worrying excessively
micro-management
Talent
Reliability, structure
INTEGRATION OF FEAR:
Accept that things change, as well as relationships

Need
Love, Belonging
Fear
To be alone/separation
Reactive response
Being needy
Talent
Creating connections with others
INTEGRATION OF FEAR:
Be yourself, fight for what you believe (be at ease with moments of solitude)

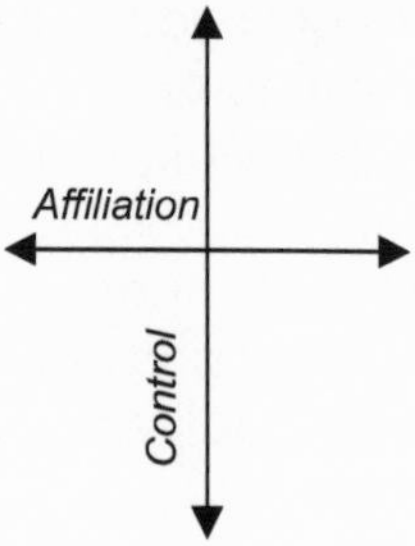

Affiliation

Control

Need
Autonomous expression, independence
Fear
Feeling suffocated by others
Reactive response
Keeping others away, emphasize independence
Talent
Giving autonomy to self and others
INTEGRATION OF FEAR:
Give yourself, show empathy toward others

Need
Variety, unpredictability
Fear
Boredom, feeling trapped
Reactive response
Resistance, rebellion
Talent
Flexibility, stimulus
INTEGRATION OF FEAR:
Find the beauty in depth and slowness,
accept what needs to be done (rules and structure)

If you were more organized and predictable, which parts of your life would improve? And which relationships would blossom if you didn't have to identify with the part that absolutely needs to remain free and rebellious?
We should begin to consider fear as our great friend. Often the experiences that give way to a personal transformation or to a process of growth are those that confront us with our deepest fears.
Once we perceive the fear, we have the opportunity of making an important choice: to look into its eyes, go through it and integrate some aspect or quality in a way that would have been impossible before.

The gift that fear offers us is to learn to identify a quality that maybe we have criticized in others before but that makes us more whole as human being.
For example, if I have always tried to live in an organized, structured and predictable way, so as to feel a sense of safety, I can learn to enjoy a day in full spontaneity, without making a schedule. If I have made independence my flag out of a fear of being vulnerable, I can learn to appreciate the feeling that sharing openlt offers.
The more we integrate a part of ourselves we have denied or haven't given ourselves permission to show, the more our experience of life becomes full, creative, light and satisfying.

COACHING QUESTIONS

Considering the four basic fears, do you seem to gravitate toward one or more of them?

____

____

____

How do you react to situations that typically scare you? (Choose one or two dominant types of fear and situations in which they occur in your life)

____

____

____

How are fears limiting your effectiveness?

____

____

____

What is the talent of your dominant fear "structure"?

____

____

____

If you learned to integrate all four talents associated with the different fears, what kind of person could you be?

____

____

____

8. At the Helm of Your Life

RESPONSIBILITY AND CREATIVE CAUSE

Why then should we transform ourselves? Why should we understand our fears and embrace them? Once we have realized that we live in a kind of representation, where the paradigms have become the walls of our comfort zone, then it is the right time to take the reins of our lives back. The search for awareness is often the engine that gives propulsion to the process of rethinking ourselves. The first step to transform ourselves is to accept our personal responsibility.

●●●

"Life is much better if we stop thinking like victims and simply choose the path of personal responsibility."
John G. Miller

●●●

Personal responsibility begins with a willingness to face any situation on the assumption that what we are, what we do and what we have depends on us. This applies even to what is being done to us and, in the final analysis, for what people do to each other.

Personal responsibility does not mean taking the blame like a weight to carry on our shoulders. In fact, it is just the opposite, it empowers us and becomes our liberation. It means accepting that everything we create in life arises from our conscious or unconscious choices. Even when it seems that we don't choose, well, we have to open our eyes and accept that this is also a choice. All that we are today we have created. But by the same principle, we can change it, if we so choose.

With this awareness we can review our past and present behaviors - whether they are functional or not, whether they derive from the drive of the Transpersonal Self toward self-fulfillment and growth, or come from the needs of the Ego - and then decide what to do with them. We can also transform our emotions and our temper because we are the ones who can choose our own feelings.

Personal responsibility is not only a duty toward ourselves, but it is "response-ability", that is, the ability to respond to circumstances and events of life. When we take personal responsibility we are able to have a greater effectiveness and mastery. First of all, we are more easily able to break the patterns of thought that prevent us from experiencing new opportunities. We feel encouraged to greater risk-taking by choosing the most appropriate and effective strategies.

We can more openly recognize victim-driven habits of thought such as blame, denial and justification. Personal responsibility also teaches us to use a new language for communicating with ourselves and with others, which includes being respectful, holding back from criticizing ourselves and others, keeping our "inner critic" and our "judge" at bay.

Personal responsibility allows us then to look at situations through different eyes, identify what our role is, and know that, if we are not experiencing what we want, we can do something different that will enable us to transform our thinking habits, behaviors, perceptions, and emotional responses. This realization this is often enough to trigger a transformation.

A FACE-TO-FACE MEETING WITH OUR FEARS

If we take a stand for personal responsibility, it takes courage to face our fears, to feel the pain of the need left unmet. We need to know that this is a temporary feeling, but we must pass through it. We cannot continue to flee the initial pain. At least not at the cost of our integrity and authenticity. We must have the courage to take ourselves to the edge of our comfort zone, to the edge of our cage, and move further to observe what happens when there is no one to meet our needs.

Even if you do not like to feel an inner upset, you can develop the ability to be with yourself, to quieten the mind and face the pain to understand where it's coming from.

Our whole personality has been shaped on patterns of behavior, thinking and feeling developed to avoid suffering. When you avoid the pain you cannot explore those parts of you that are beyond the layers of protection you have built.

Real personal growth is when you decide to meet your pain. I do not mean physical pain. When I use the word pain or suffering here, I mean inner pain, struggle. The same as what we feel when we realize that the world isn't going the way we'd like it to.

Almost everything we do, we do to avoid suffering, including the way we dress, the way we keep our bodies healthy and in shape, the career decisions we make, the home supplies we buy, which parties we go to; we do everything to avoid suffering. If you want to double check, recall the last time someone criticized something you'd bought or did not appreciate what you'd cooked. You suffered. A limited suffering, of course, but suffering nevertheless. And when you do something with the aim of unconsciously avoiding suffering, you create a weapon that has the potential to cause the very suffering that you're trying to avoid.

Let's pretend that you have an unmet need for acceptance and you have just been hired by a financial services company. To avoid feeling rejected you try to be nice to everyone, and work hard to create good relationships. You do everything you can to fit in and be accepted. You avoid taking positions that conflict with those of your colleagues or your boss. You start to dress more elegantly, you sign up to the gym where all your colleagues go and you consider changing your car. You also get involved in gossiping with colleagues by the coffee machine. Now you're not working directly on acceptance, but on how you dress, what car you drive, the way you talk.

A CEO with whom I worked became furious every time an employee couldn't attend the Christmas dinner. What's the problem if an employee decides not to come to a company dinner? What can unleash such a strong reaction in the CEO? His need, unmet in childhood, to be recognized or considered made him experience the lack of participation as a personal rejection. Had he not created his personality to obtain consideration and avoid rejection, this fact would not matter. Since, however, any refusal pressed the button of his suffering, the CEO reacted in his most instinctive way, that is, with anger.

Often we don't ask ourselves the reason for our reactions and we don't look inside ourselves to understand what sets them off. It is easier and less

painful to blame others because they don't meet our expectations.
The secret of personal transformation is to understand what triggers our reactions, to go to the heart of the suffering a person or a circumstance provoked in us and take ownership.

THE FOUR S PRACTICE TO BE THE CREATIVE CAUSE OF YOUR LIFE

To be the creative cause of your life and take full personal responsibility you need to train yourself to notice your role in all circumstances, especially in the ones troubling you. Each annoying event, every person who enrages you, every situation that scares you - and to which you react with the fight, flight or freeze modes - can become a teacher in your personal evolution.
In fact, whenever such things happen - in our fear-based programming - we tend to react in an uncontrolled way, we submit to the automatic protection mechanism of the amygdala and completely lose our personal mastery. Events that another person would consider normal, we see through the filter of the memory of past situations that hurt us. The person who stands before us then becomes the one on whom we download all the frustration accumulated over the years of living with a wound that still feels fresh.
Normally, when we give way to the automatic reaction, we experience emotions such as frustration, anger, fear, resentment, jealousy, loss, irritation, resistance, loneliness, hurt and abandonment, or we may feel helpless, lost, wounded. We lose control, we cannot think and snap with a behavior we then regret.
This mechanism takes hold of our lives. If we break it, if we manage it from the very start, we have the

opportunity to choose a creative response. The practice I suggest is what I have called the *Four S Practice*.
It is a process that you can activate whenever something or someone generates an upset, when you feel that you are about to activate the automatic reaction of the amygdala.
Let's look at the various steps of the Four S Practice, which will help us to achieve a transformation whenever we see the opportunity. The Practice of the Four S's allows you to deactivate the amygdala hijack. If in fact we are subject to our automatic reactions, we cannot have the presence and focus we need to explore the possibility of responding to life events in different, creative and functional ways. Subsequently it helps us to understand which of our paradigms and behaviors are driven by a fear-based automatic protection process, which has nothing to do with the person or event that lies ahead, but with the fact that they trigger the memory of what has injured or frightened us in the past.
With practice, it will get increasingly easy for us to move into the position of the observer and live in the moment, not imprisoned in the fear of repeating the past, nor with the expectation of meeting our needs in the future, but using every disappointment, however large or small, as a chance to grow.
The four S's are four steps to follow:

1. Stop the action
2. Step back (get on the balcony)
3. Spot the need
4. Select the option

Let's go deeper into each step.

1. Stop the action

The first thing to do – as soon as the emotions that lead us to a fight-flight-freeze reaction surface – is to defuse the mechanism of the amygdala. This gland, once activated, takes only six seconds to completely flood the body with chemical elements to prepare it to react. We have so little time to stop the process. We must quickly impose a stop. When I was a child and my grandmother saw me getting angry (perhaps yours did the same) she told me: "Calm down... Breathe."
Breathing is a powerful tool. One of the reasons is related to the fact that we can breathe only in the present, and this reduces the possibility of being trapped in the past (such as when we feel anger) or projected into the future (such as when we feel fear). Another reason is linked to the function that breathing has in our physiology. When we inhale we stimulate the sympathetic nervous system and when we exhale we stimulate the parasympathetic nervous system. The latter produces physiological reactions opposite to the sympathetic nervous system. If you begin to breathe with your diaphragm and make sure that the exhalation is more prolonged then inhalation, you are in practice moving toward a more relaxed state. Furthermore, with diaphragmatic breathing (filling the abdomen instead of the chest) we take in more oxygen to the lungs and therefore also into the brain, and so the brain will work better. Abdominal breathing creates longer and slower brain waves, such as those we emit when we are relaxed and calm.
Taking a series of long and slow breaths, in fact, reduces both the heartbeat and the blood pressure. Switching from the normal 15 breaths per minute to about 4 communicates to the body that it can relax.
A conscious deep breathing has a positive impact on the nervous system, which calms the mind

because it sends away thoughts and emotions that cause the activation of the amygdala. In *Chapter 9*, if you want to experiment with the conscious use of breathing, I will suggest some breathing exercises to induce a state of relaxation.

You can also count to ten. Since we cannot focus our attention on two things at once, counting to ten gives us a diversion from the fury of our thoughts or emotions when something bothers us. The important thing is to block the amygdala at the beginning. We are then ready for the second step.

2. Step on the balcony

Did you ever join a meeting where your contribution is expected and you become so angry that you remain silent and unable to defend your ideas? Or in an animated conversation you say something offensive that determines a separation (physical or psychological) from the other person?

When we allow the amygdala to "take possession" of us, our response mechanisms are automatic, as we have seen. And we lose an opportunity to be more effective and influence the event toward a positive resolution.

Or, indeed, our reaction sabotages our wishes and leaves us with a bitter taste in our mouth. With a sense of guilt, if we know we have hurt someone, or with a sense of regret for having been unable to act as we wished.

When I use the words "step on the balcony" I invite you to detach yourself from the situation and put yourself in the position of an observer. Imagine that your center of consciousness moves away from your body and goes up, to see things from a certain perspective.

The term "getting on the balcony" is used by Ron Heifetz, Professor at the Harvard Kennedy School of Management, to refer to the competence of reflective action which is common to successful and adaptive leaders. According to Heifetz, there is an important distinction between technical challenges, (requiring a previously established set of skills,) and adaptive challenges: those requiring a complete change in perspective, or paradigm, if they are to be successfully addressed.

Adaptive leaders manage to stay in the action and be on the balcony at the same time. It is easy to recognize this state of being on two levels when we look at certain champions of team sports such as basketball or football. Some of them seem to play as if they saw the whole strategy of the game, as if they were on the stands and on the field at the same time.

They are aware of the field, where their teammates are moving, and where the challengers are. Other less talented players, seem unable to think of anything but their own next move. In this state they cannot see where, in a few seconds, an opening will appear.

In sailing, which I am passionate about, the same thing happens. A good skipper is aware of a series of variables at the same time: how the wind is changing, what effect the wind and the sea are having on the hull, what the crew members are doing, and how other vessels are approaching the racing buoy. And the skipper is capable of directing the focus of his consciousness wherever necessary for an optimal performance. An inability to take reflective action may result not only in a loss of position in the race, but may even endanger the boat and its crew.

Without the ability to get on the balcony to reflect on the action while you are taking it, we become slaves to our automatic reactions. Sure, you might say, I can always reflect later, after my reactions, and correct the consequences of my behavior. This strategy does not always work, particularly because some reactive behaviors cause wounds that do not disappear just because we apologize. Sometimes it is simply too late to recover from the damage caused when we act on auto-pilot (as the story below teaches us). Also, if we do not learn to stand on the balcony while we are in the dance, we cannot change the course of events, because at any given moment, some stimulus will set off a predetermined pattern, as if we had just handed over to automatic pilot.

THE FENCE (ANONYMOUS)

There was a little boy with a bad temper. His father gave him a bag of nails and told him that every time he lost patience, he had to hammer a nail in the fence of the garden. The first day the boy plunged 37 nails in the fence. Then gradually the number began to decrease. The boy discovered it was easier to stay calm than to hammer nails in the fence. Finally, the day came when he stopped losing patience altogether. He told this to his father, who asked him from then on to pull out one nail for each day he was able to stay calm.

The days passed and the boy was finally able to say to his father that all the nails were removed. The father took the son by the hand and led him to the fence.

He said, "You have done well, my son, but look at the holes in the fence. The fence will never be the same. When you say things in anger, they leave a scar just like these. You can stick a knife in a man and then pull it out. No matter how many times you say 'I'm sorry', the wound will still be there. "

Training yourself to get on the balcony allows you to freeze-frame the action on hold and see all the potential paths you can take. You will have the feeling that time expands, while around you everything seems like a still image. You will feel you are developing power. The power to choose, from among many possibilities, the one that is most useful and most just. Getting on the balcony will get easier and easier, once you become familiar with this process and as long as you support it with the constant practice of meditation (see next chapter), and you will be able to observe yourself while you are in the action.

3. Spot the need

This is the most difficult step, because it asks you to engage in a mental exercise that you will find difficult while you're dealing with the event or the person who generates discomfort. In this part of the practice you have to "remove the layers of the onion" in search of the need and its satisfaction which you feel to be endangered.

To implement this step, you have to ask yourself these questions:

- What interpretation am I giving of this experience?
- What is the pure and simple fact, disconnected from my interpretation?
- Why am I reacting this way?
- What is the need and its satisfaction which feels endangered?
- What can I learn from this discovery about my defense mechanisms?

The first advantage of asking questions is the possibility of accessing the part of your brain that allows a more creative response to events, namely the neocortex. Thinking and reflecting on questions defuses the reaction of the amygdala, which loses its intensity and turns off.

In addition, it gives you two great opportunities. The first is taking responsibility for what is happening and getting back to the helm. The second is using the annoying event as a chance to see a part of you that is limited by the walls that you have erected to protect yourself and instead wants to be noticed and set free.

This is time to put into practice what you have learned so far: explore the hidden parts of your iceberg, discover the fear that your need may remain unfulfilled, face your fear, choose to develop greater psychological maturity, and experience the quality of those who have the opposite need to yours.

Some time ago, I was coaching a client who I will call Daniela. We were analyzing a reaction that she had had while working on a project with some colleagues. While she shared her idea of a workshop they had to design for a client, someone diverted everyone's attention toward a specific issue which in Daniela's opinion seemed totally irrelevant and started to criticize the whole idea. The colleague's insistence in focusing on this issue triggered a feeling of annoyance and impatience in Daniela. When I asked her how she had responded to the situation, Daniela said that her voice became harsh and judgmental and that she responded in an abrupt, almost violent way. The memory of the incident was enough to throw her back into the middle of an amygdala hijack, and I immediately asked her to take a couple of deep breaths and get onto the balcony.

We did a quick scan of the iceberg in that moment. Looking at the situation, and listening to the thoughts and emotions that had been unleashed a few seconds before, she realized that the need in danger of not being satisfied was to feel appreciated. The fear that underlined the need was to lose the respect of others and the group membership.

She clearly saw that she had responded to that situation with an aggressive (fight) behavior based on this fear. The reason was not the criticism of one detail of her idea, but the way she had extended that criticism into an attack on her entire person, and the fear it brought up of not being good enough and of not deserving the attention and respect of others.

From her position on the balcony she tried to do a scan of the iceberg of the person who had criticized her. She realized that probably, had she not had her own filters constantly focused on investigating the possibility of losing the respect of others, she would have seen what was going on in a very different way. She would have been more sensitive to the iceberg of this colleague and would have realized that he had a different need to her: the need for order and precision. For her colleague it was important to understand how that detail would affect the workshop in order to feel more confident; his questions were not even a criticism, they had nothing to do with her. It was because of her fear that Daniela had interpreted his comments as critical.

You may find this process of analyzing the iceberg a bit complicated while you're living the situation. The first few times try doing it at a certain distance from the event, when the reaction of the amygdala has reduced. Then, when you become familiar with the practice of the Four S's and when you are familiar with your needs and fears connected to them, you will see that it will become increasingly easy to get on the balcony and identify the assumptions at the exact moment in which the situation is happening. In fact, if you begin to dig deeper, you will be able to notice certain patterns that repeat themselves in annoying situations or that generate a reaction, and discover that the needs you fear will not be met, in the end, aren't so many.

Try to recall the most annoying events you have experienced in recent years. List them below:

1.____________________________________

2. ____________________________________

3. ____________________________________

4. ____________________________________

5. ____________________________________

6. ____________________________________

7. ____________________________________

8. ____________________________________

9. ____________________________________

10. ___________________________________

Reflect on the nature of these upsetting events and try to see which of the four needs was in danger. Some people identify one of these elements as being most present, for others there are two or even three needs intertwined.

The interesting part is when you manage to find a pattern that tends to repeat itself. The more a pattern emerges, the more it seems obvious that there is a need that is affecting the way you see yourself and the world around you, that "enslaved" you without you being aware of it, and that prevents you from responding to others and to life's circumstances creatively.

You don't have a need: the need has you. When annoying situations linked to the same need begin to often emerge in your life, it means you're getting signals from a part of your Ego that wants to overcome the limitation of fear.

When you have a certain familiarity with the *Four S Practice*, you will:

- recognize that when you feel discomfort in certain situations, this derives from the interpretation you make of it
- recognize that the interpretation is filtered by the fear of a need not being satisfied
- understand which need feels endangered
- recognize that you may instead choose to interpret your experiences differently, give them a different meaning and stop allowing a need to control your life

4. Choose the option

At this point, having avoided the threat of the amygdala and the possibility of having an automatic defensive reaction, you can look with more clarity at what is really happening and choose the most appropriate answer for the occasion and most likely to achieve the results you want.

When you understand the influence of your needs on your automatic reactions to others and to life's circumstances, and when you choose to defuse their power over you, you will notice how many useful possibilities there are to respond to what's going on around you.

You can always choose to express your anger, disappointment or frustration, but at that point it will be a choice and not an unconscious and uncontrolled reaction.

You will see that as you take responsibility for what is happening around you, and as you discover how thanks to the discomfort of the event you can see limited parts of you that you can transform, this simple practice will be your main tool for personal growth.

LAW OF SYNCHRONICITY

Carl Jung, Swiss psychiatrist and psychoanalyst, proposes some interesting theories. Jung speaks of the "Shadow" as everything in us that is unconscious, repressed, undeveloped and denied. There is very positive undeveloped potential in the Shadow that we don't know about simply because what is unconscious is not accessible to us.

The Shadow, like other archetypes, is an aspect of our psychic make-up that is common to everyone. Each of us has a Shadow, and getting to know it is essential to developing self-awareness. We attract people or circumstances into our lives that reflect our Shadow. Whenever we are terribly irritated by the behavior of someone or by a particular situation that presses our entire emotional switch panel, we can be sure that we are experiencing our own Shadow. The reaction is normally of disgust, hatred or contempt for certain characteristics or qualities we see in others. We deny these characteristics and we project them onto others because we don't want to be associated with them, but they are present in us and operate outside of our awareness.

Jung believed that for any quality with which we identify ourselves there's an opposite one relegated to our unconscious (law of opposites). So, unconsciously, we attract people who are mirrors of underdeveloped parts of us that we have denied but that we need for our growth. According to Jung, the psyche seeks the totality of our being (*wholeness*) and through synchronistic events (which seem coincidental, but are not) we attract people and circumstances not by chance, but for us to reveal those parts of ourselves we have denied, in order to integrate them (law of synchronicity). And if we are not able to pick up the signals that our subconscious sends us, the same types of people or events will keep showing up in our lives until we get the message.

Let's go back to the experience with the boss that made my life miserable. I felt humiliated and frustrated, and at that time, my level of consciousness did not allow me to overcome the attitude of the victim. I felt that I was completely helpless and that no one wanted to help me. Even the company abandoned me, even though I had received from many departments recognition for the excellent work I was doing. I expected someone to see the injustice my boss was inflicting on me and punish him for it. I chose (albeit unconsciously) to live this experience in this way.

Had I known the Four S Practice I would have been more aware of how I was creating that situation.

The disappointment in seeing my autonomy and my professional expertise challenged is a pattern that I had experienced often in my life. With the knowledge I have today, I can see that for many years I filtered the behaviors of everyone in positions of authority through the lens of my need for expression and autonomy, the need not to be constantly controlled by my superiors. The fear of not meeting this need was so strong that if I was asked for too many check-point meetings or to undergo several permission levels - very common requirements in the business world - my automatic reaction was to attack, as if I was facing an enemy.

What options did I have? I could have acquired a greater understanding of the responsibility my boss was carrying and of his iceberg: he was probably driven by the need to prove that he could run the company effectively in a situation where he may have felt insecure, which led him to exacerbate his control over the employees.

I could have had a mature, less emotionally charged conversation with him, where we could have figured out together how I could help him do a good job and how he could get the best results from me. I later got the proof that this response would have given a different result. At the time, I decided to accept an offer for a leadership position in London and hire, with my boss' approval, a new marketing manager who took my place.

I knew the candidate I had chosen, because we had worked together in another company in the past.

I was very anxious about putting him in a difficult situation because I expected that what had happened between me and my boss would be repeated with him. I thought he might never forgive me.

To my surprise, after a few months I discovered that the new marketing manager was getting along very well with my former boss and enjoying a freedom that had not been granted to me.

What happened? Sudden sunstroke? The truth is that my successor was not afraid that his need of expression and autonomy would be denied, and this allowed him not to make restrictive interpretations of the boss's requests. In exchange the boss, not feeling that the satisfaction of his needs was threatened, was open to granting a lot of freedom.

Imagine that Jung was right on the law of synchronicity and that our desire for growth attracts people and situations in order to offer us the possibility of transforming limited parts of ourselves.

If we can identify a recurring pattern in the annoying incidents of our lives or in the people who "push our buttons", this could offer some revelations about ourselves and about the needs that control our lives. Did you ever say, "Why does this always happen to me?"

One of the key questions to ask when we get on the balcony is "Why have I created this?" The idea that "I" created the conditions for the annoying situation puts me at the center of the reflection around what I can do.

We have the power to change things. We are not victims of others. This question forces us to see how we can learn, make changes and choose how to respond to others and to life events.

When I ask this question in the workshops, I often receive, initially, defensive reactions. "I did not do anything, I created nothing." "It is the other person who was ..." (you can put here whatever adjective you like: rude, aggressive, manipulative, illogical, confusing, dishonest, and so on). Perhaps you're thinking the same at this moment. How can I say I created a situation that just annoys or threatens me? Of course it must be another person who, by his conduct, makes me angry.

Attributing the responsibility of making us feel good to factors outside ourselves means we become victims. When we think in this way we are powerless, because somebody else must change to allow us to return to a situation of balance and serenity. The moment we play the victim we lose the opportunity to do something about it, to find a solution. In that moment we are in the hands of others. Being the victim is the easiest solution, that allows us to sink into self-pity, but it is certainly the one that makes us powerless.

Asking the question "Why have I created this?", as provocative as it may seem, means considering which part of us wants to learn and grow from the experience. This question asks us to take responsibility and to choose, instead of activating automatic reactions. We can choose to manage our emotions instead of being at their mercy. We can choose our response to the emotional hassles of life. We can choose to take the point of view that the discomfort, the pain, the events that cause us to lose our balance are a launching pad for learning, and discover that every upset can become a lever to transform a part of us that has been limited by the boundaries of our needs.

We can choose to live creatively, knowing that whatever happens in our lives we have created it as an opportunity. From Jung's point of view, we attract what we need to learn and grow.

THERE IS ALWAYS A CHOICE

In every transformational workshop I facilitate, there is always someone who cannot see how he can have a choice when he is just a victim of events. It is not easy, in fact, to experience difficult, devastating or violent events, and not feel a victim. How is it possible to take responsibility for facts such as the unexpected death of a child, or one's own serious illness? People ask me: this thing has simply happened, what choice did I have?

There is a story that I think transmits an extraordinary message on the meaning of life and the power of choice of the human being. Viktor Frankl, Austrian psychiatrist and neurologist, was captured by the Germans on September 25, 1942, when he was 40, together with his wife and his parents. He was deported to the concentration camp at Theresienstadt and then to Auschwitz and Dachau until he was liberated in 1945.

Life in the camps had little value and physical and mental conditions were harsh. Some of the prisoners were selected to be sent to the gas chambers as soon as they arrived. For those who remained alive there was real dehumanization:

prisoners were engaged in manual labor for 12 hours a day, and in winter, with temperatures below freezing, were inadequately clothed. They were also kept in an extreme state of malnutrition. They were threatened with death every day, at any time, and they were kept in the dark about the fate of their loved ones who had often been sent to other camps or directly to the gas chambers. The survival rate was very low, only 1 out of 28 survived (Frankl's parents, brother and pregnant wife lost their lives).

In order to survive you had to avoid being killed at random, you had to avoid being assigned to harder work, in the cold, in which you could often be ill-treated by the "Kapo", a prisoner like you who collaborated with the Nazis and became a kind of torturer. In addition to other dangers, you had to avoid freezing to death. The majority of prisoners lost weight, strength and vitality and slowly faded away due to the hardships and inhumane state of which they were the victims.

Frankl began to observe those who managed to survive and tried to understand what enabled these people to find hope.

He developed a philosophy of life and of the human being in which the push toward a purpose, toward the search for meaning, is the main motivation of human activity. By contrast, the frustration of this element, what he called "existential frustration", is the main source of neurosis and mental health problems. Finding the "meaning" of life is to live a life that has a meaning.

For Frankl there are three sources of meaning. The first is love. Some prisoners in the camps were able to survive the inhumane conditions thanks to their connection with loved ones. The second is work, which can give a purpose to our existence.

> A man who becomes conscious of the responsibility he bears toward a human being who affectionately waits for him, or to an unfinished work, will never be able to throw away his life. He knows the 'why' of his existence, and will be able to bear almost any 'how'.[22].

But the third source of meaning, derived from the experience of the concentration camp, makes me reflect deeply. It is suffering.

Of course it doesn't mean suffering that can be avoided. We should not confuse it with masochism. Frankl means the search for meaning in suffering that cannot be avoided, such as confinement in a concentration camp, a serious illness or another devastating event.

Our personal freedom (or spiritual freedom) is to choose the attitude we have toward the circumstances and people in our lives, and so we can choose what attitude we have toward suffering. Despite the scars of your past, the way you are treated or the adverse circumstances you may have to deal with, you can get on the balcony and see the distance between everything that happens to you and your freedom to interpret and to answer to it.

> Between stimulus and response there is a space. In that space is our power to choose our response. In our response lies our growth and our freedom[23].

The prisoners in the concentration camp looked at their condition in very different ways. Those who used their personal freedom to change their attitude toward the suffering, to make it a source of

---

[22] Viktor Frankl, *Man's Search for Meaning*, Beacon Press, 2006

[23] Idem.

meaning, were able to find a sense of purpose and survived. Those who were unable to change their attitude and who had no other source of meaning let themselves go, and waited for death.

Now look again at your daily problems, the things that bother you, the events that make you angry, the suffering you feel. Could you say that there aren't other ways to interpret what happens without making you feel a victim? Try to ask yourself the question: "Why have I created this?"

COACHING QUESTIONS

How do you try to avoid suffering?

___

___

___

If you think about the last time you got angry and you responded in a non-constructive way, under what circumstances did it happen?

___

___

___

How did you react (fight, flight or freeze)?

___

___

___

What kind of need you felt in danger of being unmet?

___

___

___

Why did you create this? What part of you wanted to grow?

___

___

___

9. Facilitating a Personal Transformation

ELEMENTS OF PERSONAL TRANSFORMATION

Personal transformation is a process, not an outcome.

It requires the presence of certain elements. In their book *Living Deeply*, Marilyn Mandala Schlitz, Cassandra Vieten and Tina Amorok of the Institute of Noetic Sciences in California identify the key elements that support transformation.

The three authors have done ten years of research on the topic of transformation, which included focus groups with teachers and leaders of the human potential movement, in-depth interviews with 50 teachers and practitioners of different practices and transformational philosophies representing different religions, spiritual philosophies and movements with origins in the East, West and indigenous traditions, and finally an online survey with more than 900 participants.

Intention

Each path of transformation requires a personal choice, the will to act to achieve change. It requires determination to pursue personal growth, to create a better alignment with one's own Authentic Self. Without this disposition it is not possible to have an open mind to the transformational opportunities occurring every day.

Without this commitment to the choice of transformation, it is difficult to stay on the path. There are times when it won't be easy or pleasant to strip yourself of the armor you've built to free who you really are. After moments of great inspiration and creation, others will follow where you perceive a sense of loss and uncertainty. Having a strong intention helps you stay focused.

Attention

As we saw in *Chapter 3*, what we choose to see becomes our reality, and by making this decision we simply ignore all the conflicting information.

The decision we take by default is to focus our attention on any apparent stimulus signaling pleasure and on any input that indicates that our needs, unmet or only partially met, are potentially in danger. Developing the ability to direct our attention toward the elements that we would normally overlook is essential to understand the weak signals or those that present us with challenges.

There have been fascinating studies which show that humans are unable to notice unusual and salient events when these are unexpected and their attention is directed toward something else.

In one of these experiments, participants are put in front of a video and they are asked to count how many times the ball is passed between three basketball players wearing white shirts and three players with black shirts. The first surprising result is that participants give slightly different numbers (some say 15 passes, others 16, others 17). This gives us a measure of the discrepancy in perception between people, even on circumscribed and non-complex events. The most striking finding, however, is what happens in the next step of the experiment.

Participants are asked to look again at the video without focusing on any particular item. It is only in this second viewing that participants notice a person dressed as a gorilla reaching the center of the field, beating his fists on his chest a few times and then going away. The participants in the study were so amazed to have missed this, that they refused to believe that they had seen the same video twice. This experiment demonstrates our inability to detect significant elements of reality when our attention is directed elsewhere.

Perception depends on our attention, which, in turn, depends on our cognitive processes. To seize the opportunity of transformation we have to bring our attention to a wider field of awareness, so that what we could not see before reveals itself.

By expanding our attention we can start to notice events and circumstances in a new way, without being limited by old beliefs or ways of seeing things, and so we can develop a new way of relating to our world.

You could start paying more attention to what you do as a mere habit during the day and begin to be more intentionally present in the moment while washing dishes, or while driving home. You will find a great value in cultivating the "awareness of the witness," that is, the ability to observe yourself and others in a non-judgmental way. And the most important ability will be to pay attention to your mental processes, toward what happens in your inner world.

Transformation has to do with getting rid of old behaviors and mindsets that have become unconscious patterns, that determine what receives or doesn't receive attention. Being able to "see" these behaviors and mindsets and bring them into our consciousness is key for any transformation. And the most common way to train yourself to do this is to quieten the mind, to find a place of absolute tranquility within yourself. In this chapter we suggest some practices to train these skills to calm the mind and broaden your attention.

Training

Just as you need to train in the gym or to practice an instrument to achieve lasting results, so learning to live more consciously takes practice. For this reason the transformational processes are usually accompanied by practices that engage us on a regular basis. By "practice" I mean the act of repeating something regularly with the aim of learning and developing experience. There are many practices that facilitate transformation. You can use contact with nature, painting, prayer, relaxation, gardening, Yoga or Tai Chi. Each of these practices can help to stop the incessant flow of voices in your mind and allow you to be present.

In my opinion, meditation is the practice which not only makes the mind more peaceful, but the oce which also most effectively promote the expansion of awareness and the cultivation of new thoughts and behaviors. Meditation supports the development of new states of being. In the pages that follow I will introduce you to a particular form of meditation that I have found useful not only to support my transformation, but also for my overall health.

Whatever practice you choose, it is important that you can do it regularly, if only for a few minutes each day.

Research on neuroplasticity has shown that neuronal connections adapt and change according to our responses to the surrounding environment, especially if these are repeated in order to strengthen new connections. The repeated behaviors are those that change the way in which our brain works. If we choose to engage repeatedly in certain activities that support transformation, we can give a new shape to our brain and our behavior in a conscious way.

RELAXATION

Before you learn the practice of meditation, it is helpful to start by developing the ability to relax through some simple exercises.

Breathing

Correct breathing is not only useful in the practice of relaxation and meditation. The circulatory and respiratory systems need oxygen to function efficiently. The function of oxygen is to clean our blood, removing waste products and toxins.

If we breathe incorrectly, this cleaning process will be prevented and the toxins will remain in circulation. Also digestion may be hindered by a lack of oxygen, and can become irregular. If we do not breathe in enough oxygen, feelings of fatigue and anxiety can increase. If we breathe in an irregular manner under stress, not only does this make us less able to deal with the situation, but it leads to a rise in blood pressure. Breathing is a

very important act of our physiology, but many take it for granted.
Before starting the meditation practice, it is useful to learn to breathe properly.

EXERCISE: BASIC BREATHING

Lie on the floor on a rug or blanket with your legs stretched and slightly apart, your toes pointing comfortably externally, the arms stretched parallel to the body with your palms facing upwards, and your eyes closed. Stay in this relaxed position for a few minutes and breathe freely.
Breathe through your nose. Let the thin hairs and mucous membranes filter toxins and dust from the inhaled air. As you breathe, your chest and your abdomen should move together.
If it is only the chest that rises and falls, your breathing is shallow and you are not using the lower part of the lungs effectively.
When you inhale you should feel your abdomen fill and rise as if you were filling it up with air. When you exhale, the abdomen returns to the initial position, like a deflating balloon. This process must continue easily and comfortably. The abdomen rises when you breathe in and falls when you breathe out. The chest does the same, but only slightly.

Deep Breathing

This exercise will help you to familiarize yourself with deep breathing. The purpose of this technique is to generate relaxation while carrying out proper breathing. It can be very useful, when you feel totally comfortable with the exercise, to repeat it in situations of particular stress. You'll have at your fingertips a quick and simple exercise to relax your body. I practice it often, for example, when I feel the

anxiety rising on the occasions where I have to speak in public in front of hundreds of people.
With a few minutes of deep breathing the tension decreases and I feel more in control on stage. This exercise is also useful before starting a critical conversation with someone, in a conflict situation or one that can generate automatic emotional reactions.
Lie on the floor on a mat or blanket. Bend your knees and keep your feet about 30 centimeters apart. Make sure that your back is straight.
Put one hand on your abdomen and one on your chest. Breathe in slowly and deeply through your nose to your abdomen so that it raises your hand up to the point where the position is still comfortable.
Your chest should move only slightly and only together with your abdomen. Then slowly exhale as though you were extracting the air from the abdomen. Your hand settles back again. Continue to inhale and exhale like this for a few minutes until breathing becomes rhythmic and comfortable. Now, breathe in through your nose and out through your mouth, making a subtle sound as you push out the air. Relax the mouth, the tongue and the jaw. Take long, deep and slow breaths, raising and lowering the abdomen. Listen to the sound and feel the consistency of breathing as you relax deeper and deeper.
At the beginning, practice this breathing for five minutes. When you get used to the technique, prolong it for up to 15 or 20 minutes. When you have finished a breathing session, stay relaxed on the ground for a few minutes and then rise very slowly. Once you know how to do this exercise easily lying down, you can try sitting, making sure to keep your back straight, supported by the back

of a chair or wall, with legs parallel and not crossed and your hands resting on your lap.

Learning some relaxation techniques can be very useful, especially when the tension builds up in the muscles, making them tense and contracted.
For the next exercise, I suggest that you record the following text as you read it with a calm and slow voice, allowing short breaks. Make sure you take a break long enough to make a slow, deep breath when the instructions require it. The recorded text should last about 10 minutes. After the recording, find a quiet place where you can lie down on the floor on a mat or blanket and let your own voice guide you in the exercise.
Alternatively you can download the free app for Android and iPhone/ iPad with my voice that guides you in the exercise from Google Play, Apple Store or from my website www.giovannadalessio.com.

EXERCISE: RELAXATION

For this relaxation exercise, find a quiet and comfortable place and lie on your back, on a carpet or a mat. Let's begin the exercise with a couple of deep breaths. Please breathe in very slowly through your nose and breathe out through your mouth. Take one deep breath. And now, another one. Nice and slowly. [Pause]

As you begin to relax, please squeeze your face into a tight knot. Close your eyes, very tight. Wrinkle up your forehead, clench your mouth closed, keep that tight knot in your face and hold that. One... two... three... and now let your face relax.

As you feel your face relaxing take another slow, deep breath. Notice the difference you feel on your face now. [Pause]

Now stretch your neck. Please nod slowly so that your chin reaches down toward your chest, stretching the muscles at the back of your neck. Hold this position for a count of one...two...three... and now relax your neck, take it back to a resting position. Now take another slow, deep breath. [Pause]

Now please shrug your shoulders.... Lift them up to your ears, tensing your shoulder muscles as much as you can and hold on for a count of one...two...three... now let them down slowly.

Relax your shoulders. Feel the difference in your shoulders now that they are relaxing. Take another deep breath, breathing in through your nose and out through your mouth. [Pause]

Now focus on your right hand. Now please close your right hand and clench your fist as tightly as you can. Keep the fist closed tight for a few moments. One...two...three... and now slowly let it go.

Notice how your hand relaxes and feels warm. Take another slow, deep breath. [Pause]

Now raise your right arm in front of you and tense your forearm and the upper arm as tightly as you can to the count of one...two...three... now let your arm relax.

Feel the difference in your arm now that it's relaxing. Take a slow, and deep breath. [Pause]

Now let's move on to the left hand. First clench up your hand as tightly as you can. Hold the fist clenched for a few seconds. One...two...three... now let your hand relax. Take a deep breath, breathe in through your nose and breathe out through your mouth. [Pause]

Now raise your left arm in front of you and tense the muscles of your forearm and upper arm really tight. Hold the tension for a few seconds to the count of one...two...three... let your arm relax. Feel how the arm muscles are relaxing. Take a slow, deep breath. [Pause]

Now focus your attention on your stomach muscles. Put one of your palms on your stomach, feel those muscles and tense them up as tightly as you can. Hold on for a few seconds and now...one...two...three... let it go. Feel your stomach relaxing. Take a deep slow breath. [Pause]

Now let's focus on your right leg. Tense up your right thigh, flexing those muscles as tightly as you can. Hold them tight to the count of one...two...three... let them go. Feel the warmth in your thigh, and feel it relaxing, the tension easing out. Take another slow, deep breath. [Pause]

Point your right toe, tensing up the calf muscle on your right leg as tightly as you can. Hold the tension for a few seconds. One... two... three... now let it go. Feel the difference now that the calf is relaxing. Take another deep breath. [Pause]

Now please curl up the toes in your right foot really tight. Hold the tension as much as you can. One... two... three... now relax your toes completely. Feel the difference in the way your foot feels. Take a slow, deep breath, in through your nose and out through your mouth. [Pause]

Now let's go to your left leg. Tense up your left thigh muscle as tightly as you can. Hold on... One...two...three... now slowly let it go. Allow those muscles to relax. Feel the warmth of the muscles as they relax, and the tension is released. Take another deep breath. [Pause]

Now point your left foot, and tense up your left calf muscles as tightly as you can. Hold the tension of the calf a few more seconds. One...two...three... now allow those muscles to relax. Feel the difference now that the calf is relaxing. Take another slow deep breath. [Pause]

Now curl up your toes on your left foot, very tightly, as hard as you can. Hold on for a few more seconds. One... two... three... now let them relax completely. Feel the difference in how your toes feel. Take a slow and deep breath, in through your nose and out through your mouth. [Pause]

As you're relaxing, noticing the tension easing out of your body, let's review the muscle groups again taking long and deep breaths while we do it. Let's start with your face. Notice how warm and relaxed your face feels. Take a slow, deep breath. Notice that your neck and the shoulder muscles are relaxed. Take another slow, deep breath. Now notice your arms, your right arm and your left arm, how relaxed and at ease they feel. Take a slow, deep breath. Now notice how your abdomen, the stomach muscles are soft and relaxed. Take another slow, deep breath. Notice your leg muscles, your thighs, your calves all the way down to your feet. How relaxed they feel, a little heavy, warm.... Take another deep slow breath. [Pause]

As you complete the exercise relax for a few more seconds. Open your eyes and, slowly, look around and become aware of the room, the walls, the floor, the light, and the sounds. When you feel ready, you can get up very slowly.

Try to practice this exercise once a day. With training you will improve your ability to relax, and after two or three weeks you will master this technique. After you learn the exercise you won't need the help of the recorded voice, and you will be able to customize this exercise and try it in a sitting position.

Set aside the time to do this exercise not close to meals (just before the meal might disturb you by the sense of hunger and just after it by feeling full) and not immediately after doing energetic movements.

If in the future you try to do it sitting, remember to find a comfortable position, with your back straight and supported, legs parallel and uncrossed and with your hands resting on your lap.

When you practice this form of relaxation don't be demanding or judgmental. Do not worry about doing it perfectly or possible interruptions. As you

build experience, the repetition of the exercise will strengthen your ability to relax the body.
When ready, close your eyes, begin to listen to the recording of the voice that guides you and follow the instructions simply and effortlessly. If you notice that your mind has wandered, which can easily happen, come back in a gentle manner to focus on the recorded voice. Once you have completed the exercise, stretch your muscles, and stay relaxed for a few more minutes. If you're lying down, remember to get up slowly.
The more you acquire mastery of the relaxation exercise, the more easily you can use it with full benefit in particular contexts such as exams, public presentations, difficult or conflicting social situations and so on. If you need help learning or applying the exercise, you can choose to attend courses on relaxation techniques or biofeedback.

MEDITATION

The word meditation seems to derive from the same root as the word medicine (as James Gordon writes in his book *Manifesto for a New Medicine*), probably because in the past many doctors were healers and spiritual leaders and through meditation they taught people how to better listen to the wisdom of the body. In his book *What is Meditation?* Rob Nairn defines it like this: "It is a state of mind of vigilant presence because it requires us to remain psychologically present and 'with' whatever happens within or outside of us, without adding or subtracting anything in any way."
There are many forms of meditation, including, to name a few: progressive relaxation, guided meditation, moving meditation, the practice of mindfulness, transcendental meditation. The main objectives of all forms of meditation are to calm

your mind, to be conscious of the present and to look for a quiet place within oneself.
The type of meditation that I present in the following pages, called Transforming Mind Practice, is inspired by the Dynamic Mind Practice, developed by Gita Bellin, and the studies of Anna Wise[24]. The main objective of the Transforming Mind Practice is to develop the ability to "get on the balcony" (as described in *Chapter 8*) while engaged in action.
This ability, called reflexive action, is the skill that according to Ronald Heifetz differentiates excellent leaders from the mediocre ones. Cultivating mindfulness in the moment means feeling free to be who we choose to be, despite the constant stress, difficulties and cruelties of life. The basic concept of the Transforming Mind Practice is to become familiar with and to master the states of consciousness, so as to learn how to access in a conscious way the states that allow for the best performance in any given task. To understand this aspect of the transformative practice of the mind, it is useful to get acquainted with brain waves.

The mind like an ocean

If we use the analogy of the mind like an ocean, we immediately have a clear picture of brain waves. Brain waves are electrical impulses that the brain continuously emits and their frequency is measured in cycles per second, or Hertz (1Hz = 1 cycle per second). Depending on their frequency, we can distinguish various types of brain waves: Beta, Alpha, Theta and Delta. The frequency of brain waves is directly proportional to the metabolic rate: the higher the first, the higher the second.

---

24 Anna Wise developed The Awaken Mind Programme using biofeedback in real time, which she later taught at the Esalen Institute. She is the author of the book *High-Performance Mind*, Tarcher Jeremy, New York, 1987.

When we are in the waking state, Beta waves are those we emit with the greatest intensity. The frequency of these waves is the fastest: 14 to 38 Hz. Maintaining this frequency is important for all the more sophisticated mental activities, for logical thinking, for multitasking. When we are at work, handling problems or complex tasks, our brain is emitting Beta waves.

Alpha waves are associated with states of total concentration. Imagine you're completely absorbed in a book, you're engrossed in front of your tablet or are dedicating time to an activity that requires focus, for example creative design. Normally you're so engrossed in what you're doing that you lose the sense of time. Or you don't realize when someone is calling you. You walk into a kind of day-dreaming state that is perfect for these activities. Alpha waves are slower than Beta waves, ranging from 8 to 14 Hz.

Theta waves are very fine waves, their frequency ranging from 4 to 8 Hz, and are associated with memory and with moments of creativity and insight: those moments of instant realization in which an idea or word you are looking for surfaces in the mind. These waves are valuable for the work of transformation because they allow states of consciousness in which a new awareness of ourselves to emerge, or when we draw connections between events and have a completely new understanding or interpretation of what is happening. When the Theta waves are present we can connect with memories, feelings and emotions. Theta waves are emitted predominantly when we sleep, but it is not uncommon to experience them when we perform repetitive tasks or tasks we don't need to think about – such as when we jog or have a shower - or in the morning when we wake up. It is

no coincidence that we have our more creative thoughts in these moments.
Take for example those moments when you're working on a project or you're mentally busy and you happen to be unable to remember the name of an actor. You try, you seem to have it on the tip of the tongue, but nothing, nothing comes to mind.
Then maybe a few hours later, when you're relaxed on your favorite chair, sipping a glass of wine and listening to relaxing music, suddenly the name of the actor seems to emerge from the sea of your mind. This happens because while you're at work the brain emits fast Beta waves, and only when it relaxes does it reduce the frequency and emit Theta waves, bringing back the information hidden in the recesses of your mind.
Delta waves represent the finer and deeper range of frequency between 0.5 and 4 Hz. When we emit this type of wave, our metabolic rate is at a minimum, because the state of relaxation is such so as not to require particular energy. These are the waves of the subconscious mind that the majority of the people emit during deep sleep.
However, they are related to very interesting qualities for those cultivating personal transformation. Delta waves, in fact, are associated with states of intuition and empathy. They are present when you have to make a decision and "feel" an attraction toward one direction when all the analysis of the logical mind would lead you in another.
During our day we always emit a combination of these four types of waves, with different effects linked to the differing proportions. For example, when we are in a meeting discussing the next project, we will emit a higher proportion of Beta waves. When we are in a relaxed state we will have a greater proportion of Alpha, Theta and Delta

compared to those normally present in the waking state. If instead we are looking for creative ideas, we need to access creativity and intuition (Theta and Delta) and we need a pattern of waves that combines all four types simultaneously.

Between the Alpha and the Theta waves a frequency range exists that acts as a "bridge" between the conscious and the subconscious mind. In fact, whereas we emit Beta and Alpha waves when we are in the waking state, Delta and Theta waves are predominantly present during sleep, except during special moments when they make a brief and spontaneous appearance and we can barely grasp their presence.

The Transforming Mind Practice trains the mind to voluntarily enter states of consciousness associated with the emission of very thin waves such as the Theta and Delta, without being asleep and therefore perfectly aware.

In this way we can more easily access more focused, creative, intuitive, empathetic mental states, that allow the best performance in any given activity. Athletes engaged in demanding sports know this type of training well. When we say that they are "in the zone", it means that they have, in the waking state, passed the Alfa Bridge - that is the range of brainwave frequencies that separate the subconscious mind from the conscious - and reached an optimal combination of brain waves that have allowed them to perform at the best of their ability.

In our complex and chaotic life, attention is directed outside of us for most of the waking state and we constantly emit Beta waves to manage our very hectic lives. Meditation allows us to turn our attention to our inner world and access a very calm place, as if we were lying on the bottom of our own personal ocean.

When we practice meditation, we relax our body and mind, and focusing our attention on breathing allows us to gradually slow down our brain waves and metabolism. After a while, as we descend into the Theta waves and - if we are very relaxed - even into the Delta waves, focusing our attention on breathing allows us to train the mind to be focused (an activity usually associated with the Alpha waves) while we are emitting much slower brainwave frequencies. In focusing on breathing, we use its natural relaxing function in an increasingly deep way. With every breath our metabolic rate drops and we experience thinner and slower frequencies. At these deep levels we begin to access places that we are not normally aware of, because without meditation we can get there only during sleep.

In our waking state we operate almost exclusively with Beta waves, and the pace and complexity of life and relationships make us accumulate stress that is deposited in our body in the form of muscular, mental or emotional tension. The function of sleep is to dissolve this stress and rest the body and the mind, but unfortunately the stress level is so high that we often cannot rest completely even when we sleep.

Meditation uses the same natural mechanism of stress release. In the case of meditation, however, the access to various levels of brain waves occurs consciously and while we're fully awake. One of the results is to increase a state of calm alertness.

In meditation it is normal to loose the focus on breathing and get distracted by a stream of thoughts.

While we are lost in our thoughts, our metabolic rate normally rises slightly and even our brain waves accelerates a bit. There is always a moment when we realize that we are following a train of thought. When this happens, we move our attention back on breathing. During 15 minutes of meditation this can happen several times. The important thing is to notice what is happening and slowly refocus our attention on breathing. Training ourselves to observe our breathing and thoughts and then make the choice to come back to deeper frequencies is an integral part of the practice.

There comes a time when we are able to focus our attention on our breathing and at the same time watch our thoughts. This means that we are thinking in a range of very slow frequencies (Theta or Delta). It also means that we are fully aware, while we are in the Theta or Delta waves. We think in a linear fashion in a state of brain waves in which linear thought is not normally possible, given that this activity usually requires the presence of Beta waves. We then reach a state of reflective action and we train the mind to operate at very slow frequencies. The ability to be in reflective action in each wave frequency allows us to improve the ability to perform the Four S Practice while we're in action and to transform the automatic reactions into creative responses.

Therefore the Transformative Mind Practice allows us to:

- *Relax and release stress*. Research done on people who meditate shows that 15 minutes of meditation is equivalent to 7 hours sleep in terms of stress release. Naturally, I am not suggesting you substitute night time sleep with meditation. Rather, if sleep does not allow us to relax completely and to fully achieve its function of mental, emotional and physical restoration, then using meditation is an excellent strategy for improving stress management.

- *Practice reflexive action*, that is, the ability to be on the balcony and to dance simultaneously, allowing you to short-circuit the activation of the amygdala and the automatic fight or flight reactions. Meditation is a tool that allows us to master our emotional states.

There is also a third important benefit connected to meditation. With time, as we gradually release the most recent stress through ongoing practice of meditation, and we enter ever lower brain wave levels, we succeed in reaching blocks of stress that are very old and which are trapped at the deeper levels of our system. In *Chapter 4* we stated that up till 18 months of age, we do not have the language that allows us to process our experiences and so the automatic responses of the amygdala during our first months of life are deeply held as physical, emotional and energetic blocks in our system. Using meditation regularly allows us to release the energetic blocks kept in Delta frequencies, which are associated with our first automatic reactive patterns. Even if we do not have any conscious memory of the big or small traumas that happened to us at a very young age, and which still today determine the dysfunctional reactions that prevent us from reaching our full potential, we can – through the constant practice of meditation – lighten up their hold on our system.

From theory to practice

At this point I guess you're curious to try the Transforming Mind Practice. We will begin by degrees. Here I propose an exercise that you can experiment with on your own. You can download a free app in which my voice will guide you in the Transforming Mind Practice.

You can find it by searching for "TMP Meditation" on Google Play or Apple Store or from the website

www.giovannadalessio.com. Following my voice will make it easier to enter into a state of relaxation and get to very slow brain wave frequencies.
After a few weeks you may feel that you become so familiar with the instructions that you can do without the voice. In this case, my experience suggests that it will be easy and natural for you to time the meditation to about 15 minutes, as if you followed an inner clock. But it would be better not to use an alarm. In meditation, when you reach the frequencies of very slow brain waves, like Theta and Delta, a sudden sound could be a shock to your system. Better, then, if you really must use an alarm, a very mild and low sound. You can always continue to use the recorded voice until you are able to rely on your inner clock.
Are you ready to make a first attempt?

EXERCISE: MEDITATION

Set aside fifteen minutes of uninterrupted time and find a place where you can sit comfortably in a chair with your back straight. If you like you can sit on the ground, on a pillow, with your back against the wall. Place your hands on your lap and keep your legs parallel, not crossed.
Remember that there is no right or wrong way to meditate. Whatever you experience during meditation is what's good for you. Do not try to make something happen. Simply notice what happens as an observer.
Now you become aware of the body. Bring your attention to each point where your body is in contact with the external environment.
Feel your back against the backrest. The thighs resting on the chair. The feet on the floor. Raise your shoulders and rotate them back slowly, then slowly rotate them forward and back to the initial

position. Fold your head slowly to the left, bring your ear to the shoulder. Return to the starting position and slowly bend your head to the right and then slowly return to the starting position. This relaxes the muscles. Your body will continue to relax while you meditate.

Now close your eyes and direct your attention to your body. After about 2 minutes start to notice your breathing. Feel the air flowing through the nostrils and filling the lungs. Feel the abdomen expanding as it fills when you breathe in and then deflating when you breathe out. You can notice your chest rising and falling as the air moves in and out. Let your attention go to wherever you feel the breathing, and maintain this observation for a few minutes.

What do you notice about your breathing? Is it slow and deep or shorter and shallower? Does it have a steady, soft pace or does it come in in a quicker rhythm?

Keep your attention on the breathing for about 10 minutes. If you realize you have stopped paying attention to breathing and your mind has begun to wander to your thoughts, simply notice this and bring your attention back to breathing. Every time you find yourself lost in your thoughts, bring your attention back to breathing. When you sense that 10 minutes have gone by, abandon what you're doing and slowly open your eyes. Congratulations, you've just experienced a simple meditation on breathing.

QUESTIONS AND ANSWERS ON MEDITATION

Relaxation

Have you noticed a sense of relaxation and calm? This is an indication that your metabolic rate has decreased and that your brain waves have slowed down. If you did not experience a sense of relaxation, do not worry; it will come with practice.

Changes in breathing.

Have you noticed any change in your breathing? Perhaps it got slower. This is an effect of your metabolism slowing down. At times participants in my courses notice an unexpected need to get more air or to yawn. This can happen if you suddenly go from slower brain wave frequencies to faster ones (for example, as a result of having heard an external noise or having drifted off into your thoughts) as your metabolism speeds up. Normally, by refocusing on your breathing, you can get back to slower frequencies. At times practitioners may notice that their breathing becomes faster during meditation. This is common especially in the West, where people accumulate a lot of stress during the day. By releasing stress during meditation, we can bring about a slight increase in the rate of our metabolism. When we have a lot of stress, we can rapidly pass from Theta to Beta waves, which causes the increase in our metabolism, and therefore in our breathing speed.

Thoughts

This is a key element in meditation. Our thoughts are an integral part of the process of releasing stress. While we are relaxed, we begin to release stress and this causes an increase in the speed of our brain waves. While we move to faster frequencies, we begin to have thoughts. When we become aware of this, we simply turn our attention onto our breathing again and come back to lower frequencies. It is rare not to have any thoughts during an entire meditation. We can be particularly tired and fall asleep. However, it is not useful to fall asleep during meditation because we will lose its beneficial effects. In this case, it is better to let our body sleep. At times, people say that their mind is chaotic and they cannot focus on their breathing. It is normal to have a mind full of thoughts, plans and concerns. It may be sufficient, when we notice the thoughts, to gently refocus our attention on our breathing.

Making mistakes in the practice

Some people judge their practice and think that they have not done it properly. The experience of the practice is completely subjective and there are no right or wrong ways to do it; meditation works anyway. Forget any expectations when you practice. The goal is simply to observe your breathing.

Falling asleep

If you feel as if you are falling asleep during your meditation, you can follow some tips. First of all, do not meditate after meals. Then, make sure that your posture is correct. Check that you are sitting on a chair or on the floor with your back straight. Keep the room temperature cool, because heat puts you to sleep. Perhaps you can open a window for a few minutes.

At times during meditation you may feel awake, alert and focused. Other times you may be half asleep. If you have no expectations about how the meditation should be, then you can relax and let the meditation proceed in a natural way; you need not make any effort.

The inability to relax

In a few cases, certain practitioners have difficulty remaining seated and still for 10 to 15 minutes and this stops them from accessing slower brain wave frequencies. My advice is to try again; at times there are days when we are really tired and it is difficult to relax our minds. If you are still unable to relax, try and do some intense physical activity before the meditation; for example, a long run or some aerobic exercise. Very often it helps to tire our body out in order to meditate better.

MEDITATION AS A DAILY PRACTICE

Meditation works best if it is done regularly every day, even if just for a few minutes. It does not have a great effect if we do it just once a week. Remember that you only need 15 minutes a day, the time it takes to have a cup of tea. If you can do it twice a day, it is even better. After only three weeks of practicing, you will begin to feel the benefits of meditation and you will look forward to your next session.

As for finding the right moment for meditation, I invite you to experiment, and discover for yourself what works best for you. For example, I practice meditation in the morning, as soon as I wake up. It gives me energy and it allows me to open my day creatively and positively. Some clients to whom I have taught meditation do it at the end of their working day, to leave the stress behind and to be fully present with their families with the right energy level. Some colleagues find it useful to meditate at the end of the day because it calms their mind and it prepares them for a better night's rest. Because I travel a lot, I find it very beneficial to meditate on the plane. It helps me to cope with jet lag.

Begin using the Transforming Mind Practice app. After a few weeks, you may feel so much at ease with the instructions that you will be able to meditate without the guiding voice. In this case, my experience has shown that it is easy and natural to stop the meditation after 15 minutes, as though following an inner clock. Remember that setting up an alarm clock or timer is not recommended.

EFFECTS OF MEDITATION ON YOUR HEALTH

The effects of meditation on our bodies and minds have been studied at length over the last 40 years and the results of all the research concur in showing the positive benefits of this practice. Scientists from different fields, using tools such as magnetic resonance imaging (MRI), which captures brain activity, are gathering evidence on the long-term implications of meditation for our physical health.

Meditation seems to have very important effects on our physiology. As you can read below, several studies have ascertained that meditation helps reduce heart or blood pressure problems; it reduces pain and improves the body's immune system, making us more resistant to illness. In addition, meditation helps cure psoriasis, and improves the immune response of cancer patients.

STUDIES ON THE BENEFITS OF MEDITATION IN HEALTH

A 2008 study at the Mood Disorders Centre at the University of Exeter, UK, showed that meditation is more effective than medicinal treatment at preventing reoccurring depression in patients[1].

One study conducted by the Harvard Medical School[2] which used magnetic resonance imaging to record brain activity while participants were meditating, observed that the zones corresponding to the autonomous nervous system were activated during meditation. This part of the nervous system is responsible for all the functions that we do not have to think about, precisely because they are autonomous, such as digestion, breathing, and blood pressure. These are the regions which are normally more involved when we are under stress. A connection between meditation and heart attacks, blood pressure and digestive problems, all stress-related symptoms, is therefore understandable.

In a study published in the Stroke journal, a group of 60 African-Americans with arteriosclerosis were monitored for a period of six to nine months while they practiced meditation. A control group, instead, did not practice it. The researchers recorded a decrease in the thickening of the arterial walls of those who meditated, and a thickening among those who did not meditate, with a consequent decrease in the risk, for practitioners, of having a heart attack[3].

A study published in the Psychosomatic Medicine journal reported an improvement in the treatment of cancer patients linked to the practice of meditation. Ninety patients participated in the study in which meditation was taught. After seven weeks, those who had meditated reported that they felt less depressed, less anxious, less angry and confused, and that they had more energy compared to the patients who had not meditated[4].

The Maharishi School of Management (Iowa, USA) conducted a study that revealed the pervasive beneficial effects of meditation on stress. A group that had meditated for four months was examined and it was discovered that the people had produced less cortisol, the stress hormone. Therefore, they were more able to adapt to stress, regardless of the circumstances that had caused it[5].

Notes

[1]http://www.exeter-mindfulness-network.org/includes/site/files/files /08%20MBCT%20vs%20ADM%20JCCP.pdf.

[2]http://www.hms.harvard.edu/hmni/On_The_Brain/Volume1 2/OTB_Vol1-No3 _Fall06.pdf.

[3] conducted by Maxwell Rainforth, Carolyn Gaylord King, John Salerno, Robert Schneider and Sanford Nidich of the Institute for Natural Medicine and Prevention, Maharishi Vedic City, and by Jane Morley Kotchen, Theodore Kotchen and Clarence Grim of the Med College of Wisconsin,
Milwaukee.

[4] http://mahashakti.co.uk/wp-content/uploads/2011/09/Med _The_Effect_of_a_Mindfulness_Meditation_Based_Stress_ Reduction_Program_on_Mood_and_Symptoms_of_Stress _ in_Cancer_Outpatients.pdf.

[5] The study was conducted by a team composed by researchers from UCLA, the Charles R. Drew University of Medicine and Science in Los Angeles and the Maharishi University of Management (MUM) College of Maharishi Vedic Medicine in Fairfield, Iowa.

COACHING QUESTIONS

What practice have you already used to calm the mind and relax?

____

____

____

Do you remember your first experience of deep relaxation? How did you feel?

____

____

____

What aspects of it did you find enjoyable? Have you had any unpleasant experience?

____

____

____

What allows you to surrender to the experience of relaxation instead of resisting it?

____

____

____

10. Transformative Leadership

The world we live in has a complexity, uncertainty and acceleration of change that humanity has never faced before. Several factors contribute to this complexity, among which we can mention the following.

Excess of information: we are literally inundated with information through many more channels than were available to our parents. Newspapers, magazines, online magazines, blogs, Facebook, LinkedIn, Twitter. We now have two working days: the one in our diaries, full of phone calls, meetings, writing reports, and one we fit in during breaks, after work, in the cab and at any free time - even on vacation - when we connect to the web. It is demonstrated that multitasking slows our performance, and yet we are convinced that jumping from one activity to another, or doing two or three at the same time, enables us to keep pace with the unstoppable flow of information and news. Where do we find the time to think and reflect?

Evolution of new technologies: every week, if not every day, a new technology, new software, a new social network is launched that requires continuous updating of our skills and time invested in learning.

Interrelations between events, people, and markets: globalization and Internet, just to mention two factors, are incontrovertibly demonstrating that everything is interdependent and interrelated. An ecological disaster in one part of the world brings consequences on markets thousands of miles away.
The unethical behavior of a group of managers leads to a deep international financial crisis. We cannot expect to be safe in our garden anymore.

Unpredictability (and propagation velocity) of new trends and movements: the development of the Internet and social networks is providing ideas and movements with a huge communication potential: think only of the Arab Spring, of its effects, and of the inability of governments either to foresee it or control an uprising of this magnitude. It's an interesting message for leaders: even if you choose to ignore or ban certain kinds of communication, this does not mean that you can control events and their consequences.

Crisis of the financial and economic system: we are experiencing the worst global financial crisis in history. We have an economy based on a metric that is impossible to sustain in the long term, the GDP. The GDP encourages an obsession with growth, with multinational companies that, through lobbying and improper financial operations, hold powers of influence greater than any national or transnational regulating body, and financial institutions that continue to use questionable trading practices. The system on which we once thrived is stuck and no longer works.

Certainly we live in a time of unprecedented crisis that is dramatically opening our eyes to the interconnection of all things and all elements around the globe.

Finance, economy, ecosystem, production, politics, religion, every life of every single person: everything is connected. A displacement in any one area causes an unpredictable impact in another. Any deep crisis can lead to the extinction or death of a system, but historically a crisis is also equivalent to a moment of "internal revolution" in a system, that allows humankind to make an evolutionary leap and reconfigure ourselves and our environment in a new discontinuous way compared to the past.

In many civilizations the moment of crisis is perceived as a turning point. In the Chinese language, for example, the word "Crisis" (wēijī) is represented by two pictograms: the first means danger and the other means opportunity. This crisis can therefore be a turning point, an opportunity to further our personal evolution and to create a new sustainable system, where the economy is at the service of people and not vice versa, where greed and fear give way to trust and cooperation, where power and livelihoods are better redistributed.

If we are to seize the opportunity of the crisis and create a transformation of society and of our system, we must support the growth of leaders in every segment and at every level of society.

The leaders I am referring to are not just the handful of political leaders and CEOs of big companies, but all those people that can make a difference in any arena, including the smallest and most important one: the family.

Each of us can develop individual leadership and exercise greater personal responsibility, discernment, inner balance, alignment with our own values, and by enhancing our ability to cope with adaptive change, have a wider impact on the people we can influence, starting with our children, and on society.

ADAPTIVE CHANGES AND MENTAL COMPLEXITY

The complexity and the acceleration of the changes we experience represent adaptive challenges. This term was used by Ronald Heifetz, Harvard professor, to distinguish them from technical challenges.

Technical challenges are those for which the competences and skills required to succeed already exist within the current paradigm or mindset, although they are not yet known to the individual person who must acquire them. To take one example, I may have to face the challenge of being able to sail a vessel during a storm.

To be able to do this, I will have to study meteorology and follow a theoretical and practical course that allows me to acquire the knowledge and experience necessary to maneuver the ship in difficult weather conditions. All this knowledge exists already and I don't have to question myself or the conventions of sailing in order to learn it. Maybe I'll just have to deal with my apprehension.

•••

"New information may add to the things a person knows, but transformation changes the way he or she know those things."
Berger, Hasegawa, Hammerman, Kegan

•••

Adaptive challenges, in contrast, require that the person develops a completely new mindset, new values and new ways of learning. Adaptive challenges are connected to transformation, either personal or – in the case of business challenges or challenges of a nation – collective.
They require us to question the assumptions and beliefs underlying our way of seeing and interpreting ourselves, others, the circumstances and the world, and to be able to reformulate them. The problem is that without having developed a transformative personal leadership, we will continue to apply technical solutions to adaptive challenges.
In biology the term "adaptive pressure" defines a situation in which the effective response to the surrounding environment is not included in the possibilities and current capabilities of the organism. This means that the body must "observe" its processes and "discern" what still works and what needs to be abandoned, and this requires a transformation, if the organism is to survive successfully in an environment that has changed. The same process should be undertaken by a person, company or organization when the contextual conditions change or when the old strategies are no longer effective.
The challenges facing us, given the complexity of the change in our times, are adaptive ones. We cannot expect to overcome them without profoundly transforming our mentality and our paradigms, without increasing our ability to support different perspectives and tolerate the contrasts between them, and without learning to be comfortable with uncertainty and the tension of opposites.
When the challenge requires us to transform our mentality, we have access to a more sophisticated level of mental complexity. In their book *Immunity to Change*, Bob Kegan and Lisa Lahey noted the

natural tendency of people to develop mental complexity over time, as a response to the growing challenges they encounter. They identify three stages in the development of the mental complexity of adults, which they call *Socialized Mind*, *Self-Authoring Mind* and *Self-Transforming Mind*.

The *Socialized Mind* is characterized by a sense of self in relation to the expectations of others. In this stage of development, people are guided by or remain loyal to the values of institutions that are important to them (school of thought, religion, political party, sports team, etc.). When a conflict arises between two values, both important, they feel "divided in two" and have difficulty making decisions. The behavior is influenced by the fear of not belonging and not feeling accepted.

At the level of the *Self-Authoring Mind*, the sense of self is defined by one's own sense of purpose and an internal orientation that is self-reflective by nature. The individual is able to maintain a sufficient distance from the social environment to generate a personal authority, which evaluates and makes decisions with respect to external expectations. Often individuals who are at this level are described as self-motivated and able to lead themselves.

The behavior is influenced by the fear of losing control and not having sufficient value in the eyes of others. Many business leaders and entrepreneurs are at this level.

At the level of the *Self-Transforming Mind*, the sense of self is beyond the limitations of personality and has acquired a transpersonal orientation.

The *Self-Transforming Mind* is capable of transcending conventional thinking and acting in ways that are authentically transformative. From this perspective, the individual can step back and reflect on the limits of her personal ideology or authority, notice that each system or internal organization is partial or incomplete, be more at ease with contradictions and opposites, and try to support multiple systems without projecting their system on others.

When we are in the stage of the Socialized Mind or the Self-Authoring Mind, we can only see *through* our paradigms. When instead we develop the Self-Transformative mental complexity, we are able to look *at* our paradigms. Here we realize that reality is only subjective and there is no incontrovertible reality that we can impose on others.

Kegan and Lahey's research suggests that a greater complexity of mind is related to personal effectiveness and a greater ability to manage ambiguity and uncertainty in genuinely creative ways. According to Kegan and Lahey, developing a Self-Transforming Mind means transcending the limits of our current thinking and deepening our understanding of ourselves and our purpose.

Unfortunately, research has shown that leaders at the level of Self-Transforming Mind are rare. Only 1% of leaders seem to be at this level. There is a significant gap between what is expected of leaders and what their minds are capable of. As Kegan says, "the current leadership capacity is not adequate to the global emerging challenges. Too few people are actively involved in a learning process of development which has a transformational trajectory."

Leaders must embark on a journey toward psychological maturity that cuts through different intelligences, and can no longer get away with acquiring technical excellence and experience in only one system of knowledge. To do this, leaders must learn to look within themselves, engage in deep self-reflection and expand their mental capacity.

THE TRANSFORMATIVE LEADER

The transformative leader is one who develops awareness and who also takes responsibility for helping others to develop theirs. She has learned to distance herself from her own paradigms, to observe and challenge them in order to reformulate them. She leads his employees with the passion for development of a coach. The transformative leader is characterized by intentionality. She is alert to problems, confident of her ability to solve them, and ready to act out of a sense of personal responsibility. Being a transformative leader means being fully aware of, and responsible for the impact she has on the world and the impact that the world has on her. This perspective of leadership requires that the leader greatly broadens his consciousness in two directions: toward what he can have an impact on (employees, the company, the community, the country, humanity, the planet) and toward what is not (yet) familiar to him, especially what he ignores about himself.

●●●

"As people clearly see that our destinies are inextricably linked together, that life is an interdependent network of relations, then universal responsibility is the only healthy choice for thinking people."
Dalai Lama

●●●

As Gary Zukav reminds us in his book *The Seat of the Soul*, "The parts of you that you're unconscious of will make the choices for you… You cannot choose your intentions consciously until you become aware of each different aspect of yourself." It follows that what we have explored up to now represents an essential path for anyone who wants

to become a leader with greater impact and effectiveness. Transformative leaders know themselves and what is around them. And they are responsible for what they know and the relationships they create, from the relationship with their employees to that they have with the whole of humanity and our planet.
The coach Nick Ross, in an article on leadership, states that to develop this consciousness leaders must include in their training four important elements:

• **transactional element**, which allows them to define goals and act in various ways so that employees can reach them. This element includes, among others, strategic thinking, management by objectives, people motivation, delegation skills. This is the most common element, and often the only one considered, in the development programs and theories of leadership.

• **self-reflection element**, to develop psychological maturity and to harmonize the relationship between the inner experience and the outside world, making it more conscious. Self-reflection allows the leader to move the inner experience (emotions, thoughts, paradigms) from subject to object. When we are inside the frame of a photo we cannot see what the photo is showing: we are ourselves the subject and so certain experiences are invisible to us. We cannot observe and reflect on things with which we are identified. There are parts of us that we are subject to, such as our emotions and our paradigms, which we take to be reality and that we are not ready to question. The things with which we have an objective relationship are the elements that we can reflect on, handle, observe, talk about, verify, internalize or assimilate, for which we can be accountable or on which we can act. To move out of the picture frame is to reflect on our own experiences, to understand the paradigms that have guided our life, and to decide whether they are still functional or need be modified.

• **transcendent element**, which implies a capacity to go beyond human experience and understand the physical world outside the limits of our personality. This element includes the ability to gain access to knowledge and information that does not come from a linear process of analysis, but is, rather, activated when the consciousness expands. This element includes experiences of intuition, personal vitality, energy, or peak experience.

• **difference-making element**, which allows the leader to develop creative ideas with a long-term vision and to create benefit for the community, in a whole variety of ways. The leader manifests in life his vocation or the "calling" that emerges from his soul. There is a transpersonal attitude that wants to materialize through a contribution made to the world. This element is linked to an awareness of the unity of all things.

THE QUALITIES OF THE TRANSFORMATIVE LEADER

When the leader is on the path of development, he works at the integration of the four elements (transactional, self-reflective, transcendent and difference-making) and brings out certain qualities that enable him to meet the adaptive challenges successfully.

Self-Awareness

The transformational leader knows what drives every decision, which needs, motivations, fears, emotions, paradigms are hidden in her internal process, and knows how to bring these items to the surface and make sure that they do not interfere with the good of the organization. She practices self-reflection and is a lover of feedback, which she welcomes with the same interest in her personal evolution with which she offers it to others. She knows that the path of human development is accelerated when we look at ourselves through the eyes of others. She is also at ease in exploring parts of herself that are in the shadow, as for example the parts she learned to deny in her youth because they were ridiculed or punished. She has a deep awareness of her own emotions, their nuances and their manifestation in her body. She knows how to use them in functional ways.

Adaptability

The key feature of the transformative leader is adaptability, understood as the ability to become adaptive to whatever challenges occur. Adaptability, as defined by Ronald Heifetz, professor at the Harvard Kennedy School, is different from adaptation. While adaptation has to do with the effort made in simply adapting passively to changing circumstances, adaptability has to do with knowing how to question and change one's own view of the world, and using these circumstances for one's own evolution. It means that the leader knows how to use external events, even the most dramatic and destabilizing, to reformulate the way they see themselves and the world. Such leaders have an optimistic mindset and develop flexible paradigms because they know that none of them is absolute but are only personal views of reality. They have a researcher approach rather than considering themselves the holder of all answers and they can change their plans and strategies on the run when they discover realities they haven't taken into account. They feel comfortable with ambiguity and with polarized points of view, because they can navigate between different realities without being particularly attached to any of them.

Courage

The transformative leader has the courage to face his own fears and walk into the unknown. His courage is conscious; it is the choice to live on the edge of his own comfort zone. At each stage of his growth, the leader must give up what is familiar to face what is unknown, without being sure of reaching the shore on the other side. Besides having the courage to reveal his inner world, the transformative leader also makes profound changes in the external reality and in the organization, sometimes without supporters and knowing that the result is unpredictable or uncertain. His courage is sustained by positive values and a deep sense of doing the right thing. The more a leader develops a personal sense of purpose, the more easily he will have access to the necessary courage for every change.

Humility

Much has been written about the trait of humility in leadership, beginning with Jim Collins, with the book *Good to Great*. In his book, Collins examines the companies that have had results of uninterrupted growth over a period of 15 consecutive years.

Among the features that these companies have in common, Collins identifies a particular type of leadership that he calls "Level 5 leadership". The leaders at this level show a strong professional will and at the same time an extreme personal humility. They focus on the higher objectives of their organization and get their egos out of the way. Humility means taking pride in who we are, our successes, and our worth, but without arrogance. It is a calm confidence that does not need to scream to be heard.

The transformative leader is ready to learn from anyone because she knows she does not know, and is willing to give space to employees because she does not need to shine before their superiors to feel good. Recent research published in the *Academy of Management Journal* shows that humble leaders are more effective and are more appreciated. One of the authors of the research, Bradley Owens, commented on the results: "Growth and learning often have to do with failure and this can be embarrassing, but leaders that succeed in overcoming their fears and show their feelings while facing the growth process are seen more favorably by employees. They can also legitimize the paths of growth of their employees and generate high performance organizations[25]".

Vulnerability

A transformative leader has the courage to show his humanity and vulnerability. For hundreds of years our culture has associated being vulnerable with weakness. I remember that for most of my life in the corporate world I did everything to look strong, stainless, a warrior.

I still have a note from my general manager thanking me for being such a "Caterpillar". He didn't meangentle creeping creature but the heavy tractor that flattens everything in its way.

---

[25] Owens B., Rowatt W., Wilkins A., *Humility in Organizations*, in K. Cameron e G. Spreitzer, *The Handbook of Positive Organizational Scholarship*, Oxford University Press, Oxford, 2011.

We are born vulnerable and we spend our lives hiding, for fear of not being worthy, wearing heavy masks that reflect what we think society expects of us. Many "warrior" leaders wear these masks. They can earn respect, but not the hearts of their employees.

Showing our vulnerability does not mean being weak. Indeed, we need a good dose of courage and inner strength to admit errors or imperfections, to take the first step when we have no guarantee of the result, to make ourselves vulnerable, to show who we really are.

•••

"Recognizing our history can be difficult, but not so much as spending our life running away from it. Embracing our vulnerability is risky, but not so much as giving up on love, joy, belonging: the experiences that make us more vulnerable."
Brenée Brown

•••

This means addressing the fear of rejection, of not being accepted, or of losing connection with others. Some studies claim that vulnerability is the key to building trust and connection with others[26].

When the leader is able to show her vulnerability, without masks and accepting her imperfections, she can connect to others and to their humanity in a sincere manner. And what is leadership if not the ability to create connections toward a common goal?

---

[26] Brenee Brown, Professor at Graduate College of Social Work of the University of Huston researched these themes. Her work include vulnerability, courage, authenticity and shame. Cfr. Brenee Brown, *Courage to Be Vulnerable Transforms the Way We Live, Love, Parent and Lead,* Gotham, New York, 2012 and Id. *Shame Resilience Theory*, in S.P. Robbins, P. Chattarjee, E.R. Canda, *Contemporary Human Behavior Theory: A Critical Perspective For Social Work*, Allyn and Bacon, Boston, 2007

Empathy

Empathy consists of an attitude toward others characterized by an effort to understand them, setting aside personal, affective attitudes (of sympathy or antipathy) and any moral judgment. Empathy is the ability to perceive the state of mind and feelings of another person, getting emotionally in tune with her, which allows one to share her inner feelings and emotions. In addition to the ability to put oneself in the other's shoes, empathetic leadership involves an ability to care about the emotional concerns of others. Caring does not mean agreeing with or approving of what the other person is saying, but it means that we can tune in to what she is going through, so as to respond in a way that values and considers her thoughts and emotions.

In a famous article published in the Harvard Business Review entitled "What Makes a Leader?" Daniel Goleman identifies three main reasons that make empathy an essential skill for a leader. The first is the use of teams to produce results. Teams are cauldrons of emotion that generate peculiar dynamics. The leader who does not perceive the feelings of his team members and what dynamics they follow will have greater difficulty keeping them functioning effectively. The second is the pace of globalization, which often creates misunderstandings due to communication problems between different cultures. Finally, the third is linked to the necessity to retain talent in the organization. Years ago I coached the vice president of a Bank in the area of emotions and empathy. Four good managers who reported to him left his team and the company, mainly because he was distant, overly restrained to the point that no one could understand what emotion he was feeling, and not empathetic. Lack of empathy is one of the things most likely to derail a leader.

Systemic awareness

The transformative leader knows that the global socio-economic environment in which he operates is made up of completely interdependent elements, each of which must contribute to a sustainable evolution of the ecosystem. He knows that his organization is part of a system that influences the way the global environment operates, and that this system plays a role in other systems, which of course influence it and are influenced by it.

For this reason he assesses the impact of any decision or initiative on the people of his organization, on the industries that depend on the organization's actions, on the community in which the company operates, on nature in the broadest sense.

This requires knowing how to balance any need for short term results with his own long-term vision so as to create value for the company, for all stakeholders and for the ecosystem.

Systemic awareness is an adaptive change, requiring a new mentality or a change in perspective. Until recently, a leader could focus on a series of targets; he was expected to develop technical expertise and excellence in guiding a team toward the execution of a strategy.

Now, because of the complexity of organizations and of the context in which they operate and the increased expectation of corporate social responsibility, leaders must be able to read complex systems and consider a large number of variables and potential repercussions related to each decision. Leaders with a systemic awareness are those who are contributing to the development of the Conscious Capitalism movement (www.consciouscapitalism.org), which wants to challenge how the business world operates. Those leaders are convinced that performance should not be disconnected from improving the quality of people's lives. Conscious Capitalism argues that the basic components of healthy economies are the values of trust, compassion, collaboration, and value creation.

TIPS FOR CULTIVATING A TRANSFORMATIVE LEADERSHIP

Keep up a relaxation or meditation practice: allowing regular time for relaxation or meditation allows the mind and the body to release emotional, physical and mental blocks caused by stress, to maintain a better personal balance, and to train your mind to be simultaneously "on the balcony and in the dance," in reflexive action. Set aside 15 minutes a day for this activity.

Practice being in the position of the observer: the observer looks at what happens, internally and externally, without judgment. It is worth asking: what is really going on? What are the consequences of this event in the short or long term?

Become aware of what happens internally: develop the ability to recognize emotions the moment they surface, train yourself to identify which signals in your body anticipate or accompany the emotion you feel. When you have trained yourself to do this you will be able to recognize when fear is taking hold of you, forcing you to defensive reactions, and to stop your automatic reaction.

Identify the needs triggering your behaviors: certain needs unmet in your early years, ended up being the main drivers of your fears, and now control your life. When you understand that your behavior is no longer useful or functional, examine your own iceberg and find the unmet need that underlies it.

Constantly use the Four S Practice: every time a person or an event is about to unleash in you a reactive behavior, suspend the action and find out which limited part of you is asking you to be transformed.

Develop personal responsibility: avoid the temptation to feel a victim of circumstance. Ask yourself "What am I choosing to see in this situation?", "What is the opportunity for me in this situation that I'm still not seeing?", "Why have I created this?".

Question your paradigms: do not fall into the trap of believing that a paradigm is your reality, but always remember that what you choose to see is only subjective. Develop the flexibility needed for not crystallizing around a single point of view.

Dedicate time to your personal development: look for stimuli in new practices or programs that develop your personal awareness.
There are plenty of courses or workshops that you can follow, from Yoga to Tai Chi, from coaching to development workshops.

Become a permanent student: learn new skills, search for a new understanding of things and apply it at the moment of change. Many of us remain stuck in old behaviors and skills even when they are no longer useful.

Find your sense of meaning: understand what your purpose is, because that gives meaning to your work and your life and enables you to see things in a broader context. Take responsibility for your development as a human being and as a professional.

COACHING QUESTIONS

What is the adaptive challenge that is emerging on your horizon?

____

____

____

How does this challenge require you to see yourself and what's around you from a new perspective?

____

____

____

Which quality of transformative leadership can you commit to develop? How are you going to do it?

____

____

____

Which action plan, at this point, would you consider in your path of growth?

____

____

____

Bibliography

Assagioli R., *Psychosynthesis: A Manual of Principles and Techniques*, Hobbs, Dorman, New York, 1965.

Assagioli R., *The Act of Will*, The Viking Press, New York, 1973.

Barrett R., *Liberating The Corporate Soul: Building a Visionary Organization*, Butterworth-Hienmann, Boston, 1998.

Beck D.E., Cowan C.C., *Spiral Dynamics: Mastering Values, Leadership and Change*, Blackwell Business, Cambridge, 1996.

Burns D., *Feeling Good: The New Mood Therapy*, Avon Books, New York, 1992.

Childre L., Howard M., Beech D., *The HeartMath Solution: The Institute of HeartMath's Revolutionary Program for Engaging the Power of the Heart's Intelligence*, HarpersCollins Publishers, New York, 1999.

Collins J., *Good to Great: Why Some Companies Make the Leap... and Others Don't*, Harper Business, New York, 2001.

Daloz Parks S., *Leadership Can Be Taught: A Bold Approach for a Complex World*, Harvard Business School Press, Boston, 2005.

Damasio R.A., *The Feeling of What Happens: Body and Emotion in the Making of Consciousness*, Vintage/Ebury, New York, 2000.

Feynman R.P., Leighton R., Sands M., *The Feynman Lectures on Physics, vol. 3: Quantum Mechanics*, Addison-Wesley, Reading, 1965.

Goleman D., "What Makes a Leader", *Harvard Business Review*, November-December 1998, pp. 93-102.

Goleman D., Ekman P., *Knowing Our Emotions, Improving Our World*, More than sound LLC, Northampton, 2007.

Goleman D., *Leadership: The Power of Emotional Intelligence*, More than Sound LLC, Northampton, 2011.

Gordon J., *Manifesto for a New Medicine: Your Guide to Healing Partnerships and the Wise Use of Alternative Therapies*, Addison Wesley, Reading, 1996.

Goswami A., *Physics of the Soul: The Quantum Book of Living, Dying, Reincarnation and Immortality*, Hampton Roads Publishing, Charlottesville, 2001.

Goswami A., *The Self-Aware Universe: How Consciousness Creates the Real World*, Jeremy P. Tarcher/Putnam, New York, 1995.

Gribbin J., *In Search of Schrödinger's Cat*, Bantam Books, Toronto,

1984.

Grinberg-Zylberbaum J., Delaflor M., Attie L., Goswami A., "The Einstein-Podolsky-Rosen

Paradox in The Brain: The Transferred Potential", *Physics Essays*, dicembre 1994, vol. 7, n. 4, pp. 422-428.

Hargrove R., *Masterful Coaching: Extraordinary Results by Impacting People and the Way They Think and Work Together*, Pfeiffer & Company, San Diego, 1995.

Heifetz R.A., Linsky M., Grashow A., *The Practice of Adaptive Leadership: Tools and Tactics for Changing Your Organization and the World*, Harvard Business Press, Boston, 2009.

Jaworski J., *Synchronicity, The Inner Path of Leadership*, Berrett-Koehler Publishers, San Francisco, 2011.

Kegan B., Lahey L., *Immunity to Change*, Harvard Business School Press, Boston, 2009.

Kegan R., *In Over Our Heads: The Mental Demands Of Modern Life*, Harvard University Press, Boston, 1994.

Kegan R., *The Evolving Self*, Harvard University Press, Boston, 1982.

LeDoux J., *Synaptic Self: How Our Brains Become Who We Are*, Penguin Books, New York, 2002.

Mandala Schlitz M., Vieten C., Amorok T., *Living Deeply: The Art & Science of Transformation in Everyday Life*, New Harbinger Publications, Oakland, 2007.

Maslow A.H., *Toward a Psychology of Being*, Van Nostrand Reinhold, New York, 1968.

McTaggart L., *The Field: The Quest for the Secret Force Of the Universe*, HarperCollins Publishers, Londra, 2001.

Nairn R., *What is Meditation? Buddhism for Everyone*, Shambhala, Boston, 1999.

Puthoff H.E., Little S., Ibison M., *Ground States and the Zero- Point Field*, Earthtech International, Austin, 2000.

Rae A., *Quantum Physics: Illusion or Reality?,* Cambridge University Press, New York, 1986.

Riemann F., *Grundformen der Angst: Eine tiefenpsychologische Studie*, Reinhardt, Monaco, 2009.

Wise A., *The High-Performance Mind*, Tarcher Jeremy, New York, 1997.

Zukav G., *The Seat of the Soul*, Free Press, New York, 1990.

Acknowledgments

There are many people to whom I feel grateful because, although not all of them are aware of it, they have contributed to making me the person I am today and to building the knowledge and the awareness that allowed me to write this book.

Only through these people and the experiences they have brought into my life am I now able to share what I know about transformative processes.

First of all I am grateful to the people I considered as mentors in my professional life and who have been - each in their own way - examples of leadership: Enrico Cogno, Shelaine Green, Jasmine Kim, Andrea Cutright and of course Paolo Ettorre, who has profoundly influenced my professional life with his presence, his ability to listen, his trust and his availability. My gratitude also goes to Alessandro Pegoraro. Our fights have taught me a lot and have generated the spark of what now gives meaning to my life, that is, learning and advocating conscious leadership in the world.

Then my teachers and coaches: Ginnie Baille, who supported me in my transition from manager to coach,

Acknowledgment

Jeremy Robinson, Michael Wenger, Judith Adrienne Lubeau, Kate Edmonds, Joannes Schmidt, Julio Olalla, John Wittington, John Kent, Cristina Mach, Roberto Sassone and Luisa Barbato. Each of them has contributed to my personal and professional growth.

My deepest gratitude goes to Gita Bellin and all the line of teachers behind her. Gita paved the way for my transformation in 2005 and offered me the ancient wisdom so I could spread it.

A special thanks to Luca Poloni and Peter Slagt of McKinsey & Company who invited me to the training path to become Facilitator of Transformation. Over those nine months I learned not only to facilitate the collective processes of transformation, but I destroyed my old paradigms and learned how to rebuild new ones. I owe who I am today in large part to the participation in that path.

My love and gratitude goes to all the Facilitators of Transformation and in particular to my spiritual family Atman: Nadjeschda Taranzcewski, Deborah Henderson, Matt Cooper, Alex Kuilman, Hendrik Backerra, Dario Giarrizzo and Joana Domingues, with whom I co-developed some of the concepts in this book.

I thank my parents for having given me life at the right time to contribute to the changes of this period of transition and great possibilities and also because they did the best they could with their level of consciousness.

Finally, the biggest thanks to Pier Paolo, my soul mate and my partner, who came into my life to allow me to continue my growth through our relationship.

The Author

Giovanna D'Alessio's professional life has been dedicated to developing individuals and organizations for over a decade. In 2001 she founded Life Coach Lab, a company focused on leadership development through coaching. In 2012 Life Coach Lab changed its name to Asterys (www.asterys.com) with two distinct and specialized operations: Asterys and Asterys Lab. With over 80 facilitators and coaches in the world, Asterys helps the most important international companies to transform their culture and to accomplish capacity building of leaders and teams.

Giovanna works primarily with top managers and top teams in the areas of personal transformation, change management, conscious leadership, people management, collaboration, engagement, personal and team performance. Her passion is to help leaders and teams to implement cultural changes and to adopt a coaching approach to management. She was part of the group of Facilitators of Transformation formed by McKinsey & Company.

In 2010 she was the first European to be elected President of the International Coach Federation (coachfederation.org), the largest international professional association that is the global authority for excellence in coaching. She served on the Board of Directors of ICF from 2004 to 2006 and from 2008 to 2011 and held the positions of Vice President (2005) and Treasurer (2008) before moving to the presidency.

In April 2002 she founded Federazione Italiana Coach (now renamed ICF Italy), a chapter of the International Coach Federation, of which she was President for a period of two years.

At age 20, she founded and managed an advertising agency. She then spent seven years as Client Director at Saatchi & Saatchi. Since 1998 she worked for Yahoo! Inc., first with responsibity for the Italian start-up, then at the European headquarters as Marketing Director for Europe.

She holds a Bachelor of Sciences in Communication and a Master in Business Administration. During her career, she attended numerous personal and professional development programs, especially in the areas of communication, coaching, psychology, leadership, personal transformation and emotional intelligence. She is Facilitator of Transformation, Facilitator of Systemic Constellations, and Facilitator of Voice Dialogue.

She is also a popular speaker in the areas of personal development, coaching, leadership, organizational culture and emotional intelligence.

In 2003 he published *Come dire di no ed essere ancora più apprezzati* (How to say no and be even more appreciated), by Sperling & Kupfer.

Transformational Programs

Asterys Lab and Asterys (the two companies devoted respectively to the development of people and organizations) offer several transformational programs.

For individuals (www.asteryslab.com):

• **Individual coaching**. A coach can work with a client to develop and improve any aspect of their life: relationships with others, personal development, work/life balance, stress management, time management, identification of a life purpose, career development, wellbeing and so on. The coach is at the service of the coachee: he doesn't judge; he encourages, supports, but also challenges the coachee to go beyond his perceived limitations, not to settle for less, and to dare to think out of the box. The relationship becomes a collaborative synergy, in which the client can generate important realizations.

• **Personal Growth**. This is a path of personal development dedicated to those who want to live in a more conscious way, as protagonists of their own lives and their own choices and not as mere spectators, taking, at every moment, the responsibility for who they are and the impact that they have on themselves and on the world around them. To master the changes, big or small, they want to see in the world.

• **Personal Mastery** (residential workshop). This is a path of self-awareness and personal transformation that allows participants to always be at the helm of their lives, to develop their personal leadership and to better express their potential. This intensive workshop, which is articulated over three consecutive days, is highly experiential and emotionally intense. It includes a mix of self-assessments, group- and self-reflections, practical tools, coaching, and feedback.

• **Emotional Intelligence programs**. These are workshops to develop a better and more effective knowledge and management of one's own and others' emotions, using international assessment models and tools.

For organizations (www.asterys.com):

• **Transformational Leadership Development programs**. In the new global economy, corporate leaders need specific skills for working in an ultra-fast, cross-cultural and complex human and business environment. The new leaders must also know how to engage and inspire the people they lead to go beyond their sense of duty, making sure they are emotionally engaged while achieving business objectives. There are a number of skills that require a high level of awareness and the ability to be flexible that are no longer just desirable, but essential to be an effective executive. Asterys' Conscious Leadership programs allow leaders to make a journey of self-discovery, to uncover the paradigms adopted and the level of awareness underlying their behavior. In the programs, new levels of awareness and new paradigms can be activated by the participants in order to increase their effectiveness.

• **Team Development programs**. A team does not become such only because it has been formed. A working group becomes an effective team when members have co-created a shared vision and developed the required interpersonal, emotional intelligence and leadership skills. Asterys' Team Development programs offer a context of engaging action, reflection and personal transformation in order for the team members to become aware of the individual and team dynamics, to develop effective communication, feedback, and conflict resolution skills, to create a greater individual and collective commitment.

• **Organizational Culture Transformation initiatives**. When we analyze the change initiatives, at least 70% of them fail or do not reach their full potential. This happen because people resist change and because management finds it difficult to support the change effectively. For the organization to evolve, it is essential to have a systematic approach to change and to create a strategic plan that takes into account all the variables that influence the change initiative, in particular the human resistance factor. Asterys supports organizations facing changes to accompany its people through the transition. In this journey, everyone is invited to and supported in taking his share of responsibility and in finding motivation and a sense of meaning that brings the individual creative energies together for the success of the initiative.

Printed in Great Britain
by Amazon.co.uk, Ltd.,
Marston Gate.